Pulford Opera

Savanna

4-17-2006

Pulford Opera

Savanna

4-17-2006

HIGH~FIBER
COOKING

HIGH~FIBER
COOKING

*Over 170 original and exciting recipes featuring fresh
vegetables, grains, beans, rice, and pasta*

ROSEMARY MOON

CHARTWELL
BOOKS, INC.

A QUINTET BOOK

Published by Chartwell Books, Inc.
A Division of Book Sales, Inc.
114 Northfield Avenue
Edison, New Jersey 08837

This edition produced for sale in the U.S.A., its
territories and dependencies only.

ISBN 0-7858-0623-7

This book was designed and produced by
Quintet Publishing Limited
6 Blundell Street
London N7 9BH

Creative Director: Patrick Carpenter
Designer: Gary Ottewill
Senior Editor: Anna Briffa
Editor: Kimberly Chrisman
Photographer: Andrew Sydenham
Home Economist: Rosemary Moon

Typeset in Great Britain by
Central Southern Typesetters, Eastbourne
Manufactured in China by
Regent Publishing Services Ltd
Printed in China by Leefung-Asco Printers Ltd

contents

introduction

Eating is one of the greatest pleasures in life for many of us privileged to live in relative security and affluence in the Western world. There is so much available to us; virtually every fruit and vegetable can be found fresh throughout the year on supermarket shelves, and almost all the ingredients for any style of national or international cuisine can be found without difficulty.

Life is made very easy for us. The drudgery and tedium has been removed from so many day-to-day jobs, allowing us more time to live life in the fast lane, to work full time as well as run a home, to pursue hobbies, sports, and other leisure interests throughout the week and not just weekends. Everything is self-cleaning to allow us more time and foods are being processed and prepared so that we simply have to heat them up.

It is the preparation of food for an easy life that particularly concerns me. Prepared and processed foods cut down dramatically on the time required to produce a meal but it is the things that are added to these foods, like additives and preservatives, and, more importantly, the things that are taken away, like bran and other forms of fiber, that should be carefully considered in terms of a balanced and healthy diet.

Processed foods are easy to eat. Not all are complete meals or convenience products; white flour, which has had all the bran removed from it, is a processed food and so is white rice, which has been polished to remove the outer husk, making it quicker to cook and easier to digest. White flour and refined sugar are good for baking, but the finished cake or bread has little nutritive value, except fat and carbohydrates in the form of sugars and starch.

What is fiber?

Fiber has become a buzzword of the closing years of the twentieth century. Growing concern and awareness of a healthy diet has prompted this. There is a certain amount of irony in this, however, as fiber used to be abundant in our diets and it is only through progress and affluence that we have started to remove it from our everyday foods. Now, we are beginning to suffer the consequences.

Dietary fiber is the substance that forms the cell walls of all plants—the superstructure or skeleton of the plant world. There is no dietary fiber in fish, meat, or dairy produce; it is unique to plants and, as recently as the 1960s, was generally disregarded as being of no nutritive value. The milling and processing of foods was therefore a reasonable idea—getting rid of the tough outer coating to reveal a more attractive and easily digestible food.

Every age has common diseases and every set of circumstances poses problems regarding health. So many of the diseases that are common now in the Western world were far less prevalent in the past, and there is an obvious link between many intestinal disorders and the processed, soggy diet of our busy, affluent society. In the less developed countries of the world—where the staple diet of many is rice, lentils, and vegetables—there is also disease, but in many cases it is associated with vitamin deficiencies, rather than with a lack of dietary fiber.

There is now significant evidence that a healthy diet—one rich in fiber—can help to prevent many of the so-called "modern diseases" that are especially linked with the digestive system, such as diabetes, gallstones, appendicitis, and disorders of the bowel, as well as heart disease. To keep as healthy an internal system as possible, it is important to cook with—and eat—as many unprocessed foods as possible. This leads us inevitably towards a high fiber diet.

The basic principles of a high-fiber diet

Eating a high-fiber diet is little more than common sense, a "back-to-nature" approach to eating. This means using fresh foods whenever possible, or frozen foods such as vegetables and shrimp. It also means using basic products that have been processed as little as possible to maintain their fiber content.

The most obvious example of this is the milling of wheat and the production of flour. Once milling was an established mechanical process, rather than being carried out by hand in small quantities between two stones, it became fashionable to eat white bread. This is made from flour that not only has been milled, but has had all the bran—the outer fibrous husk—sieved out of it. White bread was, and by many people still is, considered to be light, attractive in color and soft to eat. Eventually, commercial steam bakeries were introduced, producing a moist, spongy white bread to be sliced and packed in plastic bags before sale. It seems to me that every last trace of fiber has been removed from such bread, as well as the ability to satisfy the appetite. Sure enough, for the devoted white bread eater, there are now commercial loaves with grains added to provide some dietary fiber, following the realization that fiber-rich foods are essential to a healthy modern diet; but a loaf made with whole-wheat flour must surely be a better idea than that.

Eating for pleasure and for health

I find the word "diet" one of the least friendly expressions that I know! Eating is, for me, a great pleasure with taste, texture, and the combination of foods in any dish being the secret of a successful idea and a delicious meal. "Diet" implies deprivation, and yet another attempt to return to the size that, somehow and mysteriously, I was on my wedding day! However, I have failed to come up with a suitable alternative to the word and therefore I have to move on to explaining the

▲ Dried mango

principles of including fiber-rich foods in a healthy, modern diet. I promise it is far more pleasurable than it sounds!

The secret of success when changing from one eating habit to another is to enjoy the challenge and to be interested in what you are doing. A high-fiber way of life requires you to eat plenty of fruit and vegetables, less meat and dairy produce, and more natural cereals, grains, and legumes. It is a regime that makes sense to anyone interested in health and the environment and, more importantly, to anyone interested in food and cooking.

High-fiber foods for everyone

There is a tendency to think of high-fiber foods as vegetarian cookery. This is an easy mistake, as the high-fiber diet is based on grains, cereals, beans, and legumes, all of which are vegetarian foods. However, for most people, these foods serve to cut down the amount of animal proteins that we eat and to provide more variety in our food. This must surely be a good move for a world struggling to maintain its agricultural balance, and also for our jaded palates. New ideas and new taste sensations are more sustaining in every way than just a new serving suggestion on a packet of the same old food.

It is important that we all try to cut down on the amounts of meat and dairy products that we eat, and combining these foods with others high in fiber provides a sensible and pleasurable answer to many of the food problems of the modern world. It is healthier for us, reducing the amount of fat and cholesterol in our diets. It also means that animal rearing could be less intensive: the quality of the meat that we buy would be better if the animals were allowed to live a more natural life. It would also lead to a fairer distribution of food throughout the world. It has been stated that, even in the closing years of the twentieth century, we are capable of producing enough food for everyone in the world. The problem is that we feed valuable grain and cereal crops to animals to produce more meat for the affluent West, though that same food could be a lifeline for many people who are starving. Something, somewhere, has to change. It's not just you and your family that could benefit from a high-fiber diet, but entire nations of the developing world.

An introduction to high-fiber foods
Fresh fruits and vegetables contain significant amounts of fiber and should certainly be included in all eating regimes, not only for their fiber but also for their invaluable vitamins and minerals. As a matter of taste (which is, after all, what eating is about for those of us who are not simply eating to survive) we may prefer to cook many vegetables, especially roots such as potatoes and turnips, to make them more pleasant and more easily digestible. It is, however, a good idea to try to eat some raw foods each day—if you eat four different kinds of raw fruit, you will be eating well. Some vegetables, such as carrots and celery, make quick and easy snacks as an alternative to fruit. It is also good practice to get into the habit of eating a fresh salad every day.

▲ Dried figs

▲ Dried cranberries

▲ Dried pineapple

To peel or not to peel

To gain the maximum amount of dietary fiber from fruits and vegetables, you should eat them with their skins. This is naturally a matter of taste, but it can also depend on where you buy your vegetables and how they are grown. Modern farming methods have become extremely reliant on pesticides, which often leave residues in the soil, some of which can taint a crop. There has been recent controversy about such residue being found in the skins of carrots and I have even heard experts insist that carrots should always be peeled before eating. Is this the end of the taste sensation that is young, bunched carrots, freshly dug, washed, and steamed?

It is said that home-grown root vegetables, where you know what you have fed the ground with, may be eaten unpeeled; I think that the decision has to be up to you. I lost patience with the argument when I heard that, to be absolutely safe, you should never eat a dessert apple unpeeled.

In most of the recipes in this book, I have not stated whether you should peel vegetables and fruits—it is a matter of common-sense related to taste. Peel the carrots for carrot cake, but leave them whole for casseroles, risottos, and salads, if you prefer. If, however, you do peel your vegetables simply as a matter of taste, do remember that the peelings will make an excellent flavoring for vegetable broth, and put them to good use.

Cereals and grains

These may sound like two completely separate groups of foods but they are really one and the same. Grain is the fruit or seed of a cereal and it is a term frequently applied to wheat and other food-related grasses and their fruit or seeds. A cereal may be defined as being of wheat or another edible grain, and is also the name applied to foods that are made from grains, for example, breakfast cereals.

The history of grains

Grains are the basic foodstuff of the world and really changed the face of civilization once man set about cultivating them.

Early man was nomadic and an opportunistic eater, hunting and adding wild fruits and berries to his basic diet. He traveled around, especially to look for grazing once he started to domesticate animals. Ancient forms of wheat and other grains grew in the wild and it was found that the seeds from these could be eaten. They became more palatable if the outer husks were removed and the grains ground between stones and mixed to a paste for baking. They also kept well, especially if picked when fully ripe and dry, and could therefore be stored.

It may well have been a chance discovery—a lucky accident that changed early society—when it was found that these grains, scattered over the land, would grow again, yielding another crop for another year. However, once man decided to actually grow grains, rather than just harvesting them when he found them by chance, it became necessary to stay in one place to nurture the crop and harvest it. So man decided to stay in one place instead of being constantly on the move; indeed, he put down roots.

Basic crops throughout the world

Wheat and barley are known to have been the earliest crops and were grown throughout the early world in the Middle East. As man traveled out across the continents, he took his early crops with him, and these grains became staple foods for early Chinese, Egyptian, and Indian peoples. All crops have their ideal growing conditions, and it became clear that, while these crops did well in hot and sunny climates, they did not suit very wet areas. Other grains, however, such as oats, rye, and buckwheat, were successful. It is thought that these crops may well have grown as weeds among wheat and barley, struggling in the warmer

▲ Garbanzo beans

Mediterranean climate, but were eventually found to flourish in colder and wetter conditions.

Millet, a cereal that is not as common in Western cooking as some, is extremely tolerant of high temperatures and grows well in Africa and Asia, where it can withstand very hot and dry, almost arid, conditions. Another grain that can withstand heat but must have plenty of moisture is rice, which is grown, half-submerged in water, in the paddy fields of China, India, and Southeast Asia. Rice is also grown in Italy, Spain, and America, but in much smaller quantities. The countries that produce the majority of the world's rice are some of the most densely populated areas of the world, and rice remains the principal food of more than half the world's people.

Maize was one of the oldest crops in the Americas, but the original wild crop is thought to have died out many thousands of years ago. It must have been able to regenerate by self-sowing in the wild, but the modern maize kernel remains firmly and tightly attached to the cob, its natural carrier, unless it is removed and subsequently planted, by hand or machine. Maize is now grown

▲ Pumpkin seeds

in some parts of Mediterranean Europe, especially Italy and Spain, and in China and India, but it is most common in Africa and the Americas.

From grains into cereals

I think of grains as the whole seed or grain in an unprocessed form, and of cereals as the result of a processing operation, no matter how basic. This might be as straightforward as milling, but may also be the production of flakes or the drying and cracking of a grain, such as cracking wheat to produce bulgur. It is in the processing of grains that fiber may be lost, so it is important to know what to look for when buying potentially fiber-rich foods.

The basic rule is to buy all grains and cereals in as natural, or unrefined, a form as possible. There are very few occasions when I would go out to buy wheat as a whole grain—except, perhaps, to scatter over bread before baking. However, for a high fiber diet, you should always buy whole-wheat flour; this means that it is the whole of the edible grain, with all the bran—the fiber-rich part of the food. This also applies to foods such as rice.

▲ Black beans

▲ Mixed cake fruits

▲ Black-eyed peas

Storing cereals and grains

As these are dry foods, they must be kept dry, either in storage canisters, bins, or tubs. Keep all dry goods on shelves rather than on the floor and use them in strict rotation. Even flour does not keep forever, and I find that whole-wheat flour is more inclined to become slightly rancid than white flour. Stone-ground flour does not keep as well as regular whole-wheat flour, although I think it has a finer texture and flavor. Even if you are a very keen baker and make all your own bread, you should not be tempted to buy flour in bulk quantities—the fresher the better, so use it up quickly. I recommend keeping whole-wheat flour for no longer than six months.

The nutritive value of cereals and grains

Cereals and grains are the most important source of carbohydrates in the diet, but the amount of fiber yielded by them is dependent on the extent to which they have been processed. There are three parts to a grain: the outer husk, which is commonly known as the bran and contains most of the fiber; the endosperm, the largest part of the grain which contains most of the starch; and the germ, which contains the kernel or new growth of the plant, and therefore is the grain's source of protein. To get the whole nutritive value of a cereal it is, therefore, essential to eat the whole grain. Milling not only removes the bran, it also take away nutrients such as vitamins B and E. Most cereals contain only around 1.5 percent fiber, yet we regard them as high-fiber foods; this shows just how important it is to include them as whole grains in our diet.

The common varieties of cereals and grains

Wheat is still probably the most widely grown grain. The U.S., Canada, and Russia are the major producers, although it is also grown throughout Western Europe. China, India, Argentina, Australia, and Pakistan are further wheat-growing

▲ Dried apricots

areas. More than ninety percent of wheat is grown in the Northern Hemisphere. Wheat is either hard or soft, the soft being used for general purpose flours, containing less gluten and protein than the hard. Hard wheat is better for bread flours and for the production of pasta.

Wheat has always been the main crop for the production of **flour** for breadmaking. It contains far more gluten, the substance which creates the framework of bread and makes the dough elastic, than other flours and consequently makes a lighter and more palatable loaf. Whole-wheat flour, as the name suggests, is milled from the whole grain so contains all the nutrients.

Bulgur is a form of cracked wheat made by boiling and then baking whole grains of wheat, which are then cracked. This technique was probably developed as a method of storage, and bulgur is particularly common in the countries of the Middle East. It is most often used in salads such as tabbouleh, but I also like cooking with it—it makes excellent risotto-style dishes and cooks in approximately the same time as rice. **Wheat flakes** are used mainly as a breakfast cereal.

Wheat germ is the heart of the grain and is generally added to breakfast cereals as a highly nutritious dietary supplement. **Wheat bran** is the most common form of bran and is the by-product of milling white flour. It is rich in fiber and is added to breads or sold to be added to cereals.

Semolina and **couscous** are both wheat products. Semolina is a meal ground from durum wheat, a particularly hard form of wheat used for pasta-making. Semolina is used in milk puddings and readily absorbs liquid. I scatter it lightly under fish or meat that is to be cooked wrapped in pastry —the semolina absorbs any juices and prevents the pastry from becoming soggy during cooking. Couscous is pellets of processed fine and coarse semolinas mixed together and then sifted into shape. It has given its name to a dish, when it is steamed over a stew with which it is served.

Barley is available as a whole grain, which is known as **pot barley**, to be used in stews. It may take up to three hours to cook and never really becomes soft and tender. **Pearl barley** is the husked, polished berry and is traditionally used in soups, both for flavor and as a thickener. **Barley flour** is used in many eastern European countries to make bread, but it gives a rather grey loaf of a dense texture, less palatable than a wheat loaf. It has a sweet flavor, however, and is a useful ingredient in a mixed grain loaf when combined with wheat and rye flours. Barley may also be used to make a form of oatmeal, but is most commonly associated with the brewing industry, where it is used in the production of malt for both beers and whiskey.

Rye is widely grown and used in northern European and Scandinavian countries, as it is tolerant of cold weather and acid soils. Until the nineteenth century, **rye flour** was more commonly used in some areas for bread than wheat, but as soon as white bread became fashionable, so did wheat flour. Rye flour is used to make "black" breads and crackers. It does not have the same gluten content as wheat so the resulting yeasted breads are heavier and do not rise as much. **Crackers** were originally made to prolong the storage life of the rye crop. Short summers in northern Europe meant that the rye often had to be harvested before it was really ripe, and the unripe grain did not store well, being too full of moisture. Roughly ground and baked into slabs, it was found that these fiber-rich crackers kept well and could be stored right through the long winter months. Some rye is grown in North America and it is often fermented to make rye whiskey. Rye is darker in color than wheat and has a stronger flavor, although it is sometimes processed into a

▲ Bulgur

▲ Pearl barley

white flour which then loses most of the distinctive rye flavor.

Somehow **oats** have a far more rustic image than the other grains and cereal crops. They are a hardy crop, and are often made into a gruel or mush. Oats are a soft grain and are therefore not suitable for milling into flour. The crop is adaptable and is thought to have been grown in ancient Mesopotamia and Abyssinia, both of which are very warm. It would have provided useful cover for more tender plants, shielding them from the sun. Oats are now usually grown in colder climates in the Northern Hemisphere, in the U.S., Europe, and Russia.

Oats are a good source of iron, potassium, and vitamin B, as well as being rich in fiber and carbohydrates, with some protein and fat. **Oat flakes,** or **rolled oats**, are used for baking and for oatmeal, a warming breakfast dish (especially good with brown sugar on very cold days!). **Oatmeal** or **Irish oatmeal** (also widely used in Scotland) is milled in various grades and may be used for baking, especially oatcakes and the famous Scottish sausage, haggis. **Oat bran** is the fiber-rich

outer casing of the oats. It can be added to most breakfast cereals or mixed with rolled oats for hot oatmeal.

Millet is thought of by many people as little more than bird food, yet it is widely grown in Africa and in some countries in Asia and Europe. It does make excellent savory baked goods—it has a creamy texture and must be boiled before being turned into a finished dish—I have used it for rissoles and savory baked goods. It may also be used as a thickener, especially for soups and stews, in which case it should be cooked in the stock of the dish. It does swell considerably, so don't be tempted to add too much.

Corn or **maize** is the biggest crop in America, which grows over forty percent of the world's total production. It is colloquially known as corn on the cob and grows very high—I have worked in corn fields in southern England where the crop has been taller than I am. The terms corn and maize are interchangeable; therefore, corn flour and maize flour are the same basic product, although they may vary in color.

Corn, when on the cob, is very high in dietary

▲ Granola

▲ Bread crumbs

fiber and requires a good deal of chewing! Dripping with melted butter, it makes an excellent appetizer, although it is not easy to eat elegantly!

Corn is available processed as **cornstarch**, a very fine flour used for thickening liquids for sauces, stews, and soups. It is generally white. **Corn meal** and **polenta** are not quite so finely ground and are usually yellow in color. Polenta is produced in Italy and is generally made into a solid, oatmeal-like substance which is delicious sliced or baked (preferably with a cheese topping). Corn or maize flour is used extensively throughout the U.S. for bread and gives a much sweeter flavor than wheat flour.

Hominy and **grits** are common foods in the South. The first is the dried corn kernels, also widely available in cans. They should be soaked to reconstitute them and then baked or fried, although I prefer to use them in casseroles, especially pork. Even when soaked overnight, hominy may take five hours of simmering to soften. Grits are ground hominy and cook much more quickly; they are often served as a mash with bacon and eggs.

Blue cornmeal is highly valued because of its unusual appearance. The flour is usually made into tortilla chips or sold for making pancakes. It really is blue and comes from a dark blue strain of corn. Apart from culinary uses, it may be found in some cosmetic products, such as face scrubs and deep cleansers.

Popcorn is a particularly hard corn kernel which turns itself inside out when cooked in a dry, covered pan. The pan should be well sealed, otherwise the exploding corn may cover your kitchen. I think the benefits from the fiber content of popcorn are usually drowned out by the amount of butter or salt used to coat it.

One of the more unusual grains available is **buckwheat**, which is really the fruit or seed of a plant closely related to rhubarb and sorrel, and therefore not really a grain at all. It does, however,

cook like a grain. It is available both raw and roasted, the latter having a deeper and slightly more palatable flavor. It is rich in vitamins A and B and also calcium, as well as carbohydrates. Buckwheat is available as groats (grains) or as flour. The flour, which is an unusual gray color, is used for pancakes, crêpes, and muffins; generally, I find bread made with buckwheat very unappealing and not to my taste. The most common use for buckwheat flour is in the making of blinis—little yeasted pancakes often served with sour cream and smoked salmon and common in Russia, where they are also served with caviar.

Rice is the staple food of about half the population of the world and is grown on every continent except Antarctica. It is a cereal grass and grows in water on marshy flooded land, usually known as paddy-fields, in conditions in which other grains—such as barley and wheat—would not survive.

Rice is native to India and Indo-China but its cultivation quickly spread throughout the East. Ancient Chinese records speak of planting ceremonies after permission to grow rice had been granted by the emperor. The term "paddy-field" actually comes from the Chinese word for unhusked rice grains.

The Romans brought rice back to Italy following their travels to the East and it was originally grown in the flooded plains of the Po Valley. Indeed, risotto rice is still grown there today. As the Roman Empire expanded, so too did the cultivation of rice, moving to Spain and parts of Africa. Today, there is also a great deal of rice grown in the U.S., but this really came about by accident when a spice ship from Madagascar, bound for England, was blown off course, and ended up in Charlestown, South Carolina. In gratitude to his hosts for their hospitality, the captain of the ship presented them with some of his cargo of rough seed rice, which has flourished in the South ever since.

▲ Buckwheat

▲ Wild rice

▲ Brown rice

The nutritive value of rice

Rice is not fattening; like pasta, it's the food you serve with it that can do the damage! All rices are valuable sources of B-group vitamins and minerals, especially potassium and phosphorus. Brown rice contains both more fiber and more protein than white rice and also contains calcium and iron.

Brown rice is simply the unmilled or unpolished grain, so all varieties of rice should be available as brown rice. It is quite easy to find brown long grain, short grain, and basmati rices, and brown arborio or risotto rice is sometimes available in very good health stores. Brown rice takes longer to cook than white; never add salt to the water during cooking as it may toughen the grain. The length of cooking time may be slightly shortened by soaking the rice in the measured amount of water before cooking.

Instant or converted rice is partially steamed before the milling process. This forces the nutrients from the bran into the rice grain so that they are retained during milling. Instant brown rice is now widely available.

There are many other types of rice, most of which are most commonly available in their white or polished forms. Among my favorites are **arborio** and **carnarolli** rice, which are both forms of **risotto** rice, and **basmati**, the finest grain of all the rices, which is grown in the foothills of the Himalayas. **Camargue red rice** is an unpolished rice grown in very small quantities in southern France, which has a very nutty flavor as well as a very distinctive color.

Wild rice is actually the seed from an aquatic grass grown in the northern U.S. and in Canada. It has very long, slender grains, and I think it smells like Darjeeling tea while it is cooking. Originally very expensive, as it was hand-harvested in a boat, wild rice is now being grown commercially, which is helping both availability and cost, although the cultivated grains do not have quite the same flavor as the truly wild variety.

▲ Green lentils

▲ Navy beans

▲ Mung beans

Wild rice has a far higher nutritive value than either of the two main cereal crops, regular rice and wheat. Its protein contains all nine of the essential amino acids, making it a complete protein. Because it is unpolished, it is also very rich in fiber.

Rice bran is the husk of the rice, removed during milling. It is not a common product except in countries where rice is processed, but it is used as a supplement to breakfast cereals. Flaked rice cooks quickly and is used mainly in puddings, although it is often added to granolas. **Rice flour** is used especially in Chinese cookery to make rice noodles, but can also be used to thicken sauces and in cakes and pastries for people who are allergic to wheat flour. It is very fine and is often used in the cosmetics industry as a base for eye shadows and other makeup. **Ground rice** is the rice equivalent of semolina, fine and grainy and used for puddings and cookies, especially shortbread.

Beans: dried foods rich in nutrients

Beans and legumes are not only a good source of fiber in the diet—red kidney beans, for example, contain 4.5 percent fiber and as much protein as meat (24 percent), and much the same is true of garbanzo beans and lentils—all beans also contain vitamins, especially B-group, and minerals, notably iron. There is a wide variety of beans in different shapes and colors, making them an invaluable part of our diet. From the eating angle, however, most of them taste remarkably similar! Garbanzo and adzuki beans are outstanding in their flavor, in my opinion. After that, the choice is governed by appearance, the dish being made, and the length of cooking time available.

In the recipes that I have included in this book, I have used my favorite beans, the ones that I generally have in my cupboard. I have not included any recipes for soy beans, for example, as I do not keep them at home. They could, however,

▲ Red lentils

be used in any of the recipes calling for a similar size of bean; for example, navy beans or black-eyed peas.

Adzuki beans are common in Chinese and Japanese cooking and grow in both countries. They are a rich, nutty brown in color and very small. The most obvious feature of the beans is their slightly sweet flavor—they are often used in sweet dishes, and I have included them in a savory casserole and a delicious sweet dessert cobbler.

Mung beans are a similar size to adzuki beans but are green in color. They may be sprouted for a salad vegetable, and are sometimes ground into flour. They are most commonly used in Chinese and Indian cookery, but I have used them in a recipe for vegetable pasties.

Lentils are unique among beans, as they do not require soaking before cooking. This makes them an instant food, and red lentils are often dropped in food parcels to disaster areas because they can be cooked up into a paste or *dal* immediately, providing protein and other valuable nutrients. Lentils are red, yellow, green, brown, or almost black, the latter being *puy* lentils, beloved of the French. I use mainly red and green lentils, and you will find both in recipes in this book—the lentil soufflé is delicious and most unusual.

There are a number of medium-sized white beans that are suitable for general cookery. **Haricots** are considered to be the basic bean of Europe and keep their shape well when cooked in casseroles, the most famous of which is cassoulet.

▲ Cannellini beans

▲ Red kidney beans

Navy beans were probably the original baked bean and are widely used in America, although I find them very difficult to tell apart from haricots —for all intents and purposes, they are the same. **Cannellini beans** are Italian white beans, slightly more elongated than navy beans, and are often used with tuna fish to make antipasta, although I have used **flageolets** for my tuna bean salad. They are also a member of the kidney bean family, but have an attractive green color. They are generally available canned and are a very good store cupboard standby.

Garbanzo beans are called chana in India and chick peas in many other countries. They are large, pea-shaped beans that are used extensively in Mediterranean and Middle Eastern cookery. They have a distinctive nutty flavor and are used in casseroles and in dips, the most famous of which is hummus. Garbanzo beans are a natural partner to sesame seeds and are often used with tahini, a paste of ground sesame.

Other medium-sized beans include **black beans**, used in South American cookery (these are different from the small, round black beans, fermented and used in Japanese cookery) and **pinto beans**, which are brown in color and are the traditional beans for use in Mexican dishes, including chili con carne. They also have the distinction of cooking more quickly than most other beans. **Borlotti beans** are an oval brown bean speckled with pink. They are attractive in appearance and are used in Italian cookery, especially in salads. **Dutch brown beans** are another variety of the common kidney bean but

are not as widely available as many other varieties. **Red kidney beans** are the meat of the kidney bean family: large beans that are widely used because of their color. Kidney beans should always be boiled vigorously for the first ten minutes of their cooking time, in order to destroy any toxins that may be in the beans. This is a good rule to follow for all beans.

Broad beans are often called **fava beans** in their fresh state, but the same name is also given to butter beans, especially the small variety from Madagascar. **Lima beans** are usually large and white in color, and have a sweet, creamy flavor. Although they are often associated with school dinners, I like them a lot and use them in both soups and casseroles.

There are two other beans that are not so common but are worth mentioning. **Ful mesdames** are an Egyptian bean, and a casserole of these beans is to Egypt what roast beef and Yorkshire pudding are to England: a national dish. They have a very dedicated following and I used to sell them canned in great quantities when I owned a delicatessen. **Pigeon peas** are similar in size to black-eyed peas or beans, and have an earthy flavor. They are sometimes called gunga peas and are widely used throughout the Caribbean, especially for any dish where they are accompanied by rice.

Other fiber-rich foods to include in your diet
Pasta is a derivative of wheat and is also a high-fiber food. Whole-wheat pasta contains more fiber than other types, but it can be very similar to

▲ Pinto beans

▲ Pecans

cardboard in both taste and texture. I make good whole-wheat pasta, but if I do not want to make my own I prefer to buy white pasta for texture and color. It is interesting to note how few varieties of commercial whole-wheat pasta are available now— there is obviously a limit to eating what is supposed to do you good!

Nuts are a valuable source of dietary fiber and should always be included in a mixed diet. They are, however, very high in fat, so care should be taken to eat them only in moderation. They typically contain 2 percent fiber, and 59 percent fat. Be warned!

Changing to a high-fiber diet

High-fiber eating makes sense when you consider the benefits of eating food in as natural a state as possible. I, however, am not a dietician and cannot advise you as to quantities of fiber and the right diet for you. I can only say that to introduce high-fiber foods gradually into your everyday diet will be an adventure of flavors and textures, and I have found that I feel brighter when I am eating foods that are a challenge to my taste buds and to my digestive system.

Not every food that you eat has to be high-fiber —you may chose to keep to white pasta if you change to whole-wheat bread and start eating more fresh fruits, salads, and vegetables. As with any eating regime, it is a good idea to eat a wide variety of foods—do not rely on sprinkling bran over everything to increase your fiber intake. This will not be good for your taste buds or for your digestion.

Using the recipes in this book

I have included many varied recipes in this book but, even so, they are really only an introduction to the huge selection of dishes that can be made within the bounds of a high-fiber diet. High-fiber does not necessarily mean vegetarian, but many of the recipes are suitable for those who do not eat meat. I do believe that we need meat or fish at only one meal of each day, so eating more vegetarian foods is not only healthy but also socially and environmentally correct.

Most of the recipes are simple and straightforward and need no special attention. However, high-fiber baking includes more bran and moisture-hungry foods than regular baking, so you will find it advisable to make such mixtures a degree or so wetter.

I like to use butter and olive oil in my kitchen at home. In most of these recipes, sunflower margarine may be used in place of butter, but always use it straight from the refrigerator. You may use your own choice of fat or oil, but always consider the flavor of the finished dish.

A good diet should not only be high in fiber but also low in fat and sugars. Cakes and cookies should be treats and not everyday foods, and the amount of extra fat added to foods should be kept to a minimum.

Some of these dishes may be very different from the foods that you have been used to eating for many years. I hope that you will enjoy trying them, and that you will discover a whole new culinary repertoire that will not only be good for your health, but will taste good as well.

soups and chowders

A high-fiber soup can easily be a meal in itself, so take care when menu planning, especially for a three or four course meal. Many of these soups and chowders are made with root vegetables or beans which give a thick texture, especially if the soup is blended at the end of cooking. Thin them down if you wish by adding extra broth or milk, but remember that soups are essentially comfort food and therefore I prefer them thick.

Soups should always be served piping hot or very cold; a tepid soup is a disaster. Do not boil soups that have had light cream or fruit juices, such as orange or lemon, added to them—the cream may curdle and the flavor of the fruit will become tainted. Chilled soups are always better served over crushed ice.

The secret of any successful soup is the flavor of the broth used in its making. Broths are not difficult to prepare and really consist of bones and vegetable peelings, a few herbs, and some peppercorns. I collect all my onion skins, carrot scrapings, and other vegetable waste, place them in a large pan with plenty of water, herbs, and a light seasoning of salt. Bring to a boil then simmer very slowly for two to three hours, until a rich, dark liquor is produced. Strain the broth then season it lightly. The broth may be reduced to intensify the flavor, in which case it should not be seasoned until it has been boiled. Never cover the pan or the resulting broth may be musty in flavor and cloudy. This will not make your kitchen steamy during cooking, however, as the broth should be simmered very slowly, with just an occasional bubble breaking the surface.

Sausage, Apple, and Pasta Soup

Serves 4

This is definitely a main course soup! If you don't eat meat, serve cubed cheese, which will start to melt in the soup. I have used standard pork sausages, but a spicier variety could be used.

2 Tbsps vegetable oil
1 pound pork sausages
1 onion, chopped finely
1 red bell pepper, seeded and chopped
2 cups dry cider
4 cups broth
Salt and freshly ground black pepper
½ tsp ground nutmeg
1 cup whole-wheat macaroni
1 large tart green apple, chopped finely
½ cup grated Cheddar cheese (optional)

Heat the oil in a large pan, then add the sausages and cook quickly until browned on all sides. Add the onion and pepper and cook more slowly for 3 to 4 minutes, until the vegetables are soft.

Add the cider and broth to the pan with the seasonings and bring to a boil. Simmer the soup for 30 minutes, then remove the sausages with a slotted spoon. Add the macaroni and simmer for a further 10–12 minutes, or until the pasta is cooked. Slice the sausages while the macaroni is cooking then return the meat to the pan. Add the apple just before the pasta is cooked—do not simmer it for more than 2 minutes.

Season the soup to taste then serve immediately, with or without grated cheese.

Parsnip and Apple Soup

Serves 4–6

Curried parsnip is one of the new generation of classic soups. I like to add a tart green apple to the mixture—its sharpness gives a real punch to the flavor of the soup.

1 onion, chopped
1 Tbsp sunflower oil
1 tsp mild curry powder
1 pound parsnips, chopped
1 tart green apple, peeled, cored, and sliced
5 cups well-flavored vegetable broth
Salt and freshly ground black pepper
Juice of ½ a lemon
Freshly chopped parsley or cilantro to garnish

Cook the onion in the oil for 4 to 5 minutes until soft, then stir in the curry powder with the parsnips. Cook for a further 2 to 3 minutes before adding the apple and broth. Bring to a boil, then simmer for 30 minutes or until the parsnip is soft.

Allow the soup to cool slightly, then purée until smooth in a blender or food processor. Rinse the pan and return the soup to it, adding sufficient water to thin the soup if necessary. Reheat gently, then season to taste with salt and pepper. Add the lemon juice just before serving and garnish with parsley or cilantro.

Parsnip and Apple Soup ▶

Roasted Pumpkin and Smoked Mussel Soup

Serves 6

A luxurious soup that is just as good for a lazy lunch or as a sophisticated starter. Mussels are easy to smoke at home if you are unable to buy them in your local store.

½ small pumpkin or 1 medium firm-fleshed squash
Freshly ground black pepper
3 Tbsps olive oil
1 leek, sliced finely
2 stalks celery, trimmed and sliced
1 carrot, sliced
2 tsps ground coriander
3–4 sprigs fresh thyme
1 bay leaf
4 cups well-flavored vegetable broth
2 cups milk
salt
1 cup smoked mussels
Freshly chopped parsley

Preheat oven to 425°F. Cut the pumpkin into slices about 1½ to 2 inches wide and place them in a roasting pan. You will need 6 slices. Season lightly with pepper then brush the flesh with olive oil. Bake in the preheated oven for about 30 minutes, until the pumpkin is tender. Scoop the flesh from the skin and place to one side.

Heat 2 tablespoons of olive oil in a large pan; add the leek, celery, and carrot and cook slowly until soft. Stir in the ground coriander and cook slowly for a further minute. Add the pumpkin flesh to the pan with the thyme and bay leaf, then pour in the broth. Bring the soup to a boil then cover and simmer slowly for 35–40 minutes.

Allow the soup to cool slightly then purée until smooth in a blender or food processor. Rinse the pan then return the soup to it with the milk and bring slowly to simmering point. Season well with salt and pepper then add the smoked mussels and heat for another minute or two. Serve garnished with parsley.

Roasted Pumpkin and Smoked Mussel Soup ▶

Armenian Soup

Serves 6

A spicy lentil soup, sweetened and thickened with apricots and golden raisins. Ginger, cumin, and cinnamon make an exotic trio of seasonings.

soups and chowders

1 large onion, chopped finely
2 Tbsps olive oil
1 tsp ground ginger
1 tsp ground cumin
½ tsp ground cinnamon
2 tomatoes, diced
1 cup red lentils
6 cups well-flavored vegetable broth
Salt and freshly ground black pepper
½ cup ready-to-eat dried apricots, roughly chopped
⅓ cup golden raisins
Sour cream (optional)

Cook the onion in the oil in a large pan until soft, then add the spices and cook for 1 minute over low heat. Add the tomatoes and lentils, then stir in the broth and bring the soup slowly to a boil. Season well, add the dried fruits, then cover and simmer for 30 minutes, until the lentils and vegetables are soft.

Season the soup to taste. It may be puréed if preferred, then thinned down with a little extra broth or water. Serve with a dollop of sour cream.

Lebanese Couscous Soup

Serves 6

Couscous, tiny grains made from semolina, is usually steamed over a stew or broth. In this recipe, I have used the couscous to thicken a richly spiced onion soup.

4 large onions, sliced finely
3 cloves garlic, sliced finely
2 Tbsps vegetable oil
1 Tbsp butter
1 red chile, seeded and chopped finely
1 tsp mild chile powder
½ tsp ground turmeric
1 tsp ground coriander
Salt and freshly ground black pepper
8 cups well-flavored vegetable or chicken broth
⅓ cup couscous
Freshly chopped cilantro to garnish

Cook the onions and garlic in the oil and butter until well browned. This will take about 15 minutes over a medium high heat. You must let the onions brown to achieve a rich color for the finished soup.

Stir in the chopped chile and the spices and cook over a low heat for a further 1 to 2 minutes before adding the broth. Season lightly then bring to a boil. Cover and simmer for 30 minutes.

Stir the couscous into the soup, return to a boil, and simmer for a further 10 minutes. Season to taste then garnish with cilantro and serve immediately.

Lebanese Couscous Soup ▶

Lima Bean and Parsnip Soup

Serves 6

A sweet, creamy soup, subtly flavored with nutmeg. Use freshly grated nutmeg if possible—the flavor is so much better than with powdered.

1 onion, chopped
2 Tbsps oil
1 clove garlic
1½ cups diced parsnip
1 cup lima beans, soaked overnight
4½ cups well-flavored vegetable broth
Salt and freshly ground black papper
Freshly grated nutmeg
1 cup milk
2 slices whole-wheat bread
2 Tbsps butter or margarine
1 Tbsp freshly chopped parsley

Cook the onion in the oil until soft, then add the garlic and parsnip and continue cooking until the parsnip starts to brown.

Drain the soaked lima beans and rinse them thoroughly under running water. Add the beans to the pan with the broth, some salt, pepper, and freshly grated nutmeg. Bring the soup to a boil, then cover and simmer slowly for about an hour, until the beans are tender.

Allow the soup to cool slightly then purée it until smooth in a blender or food processor. Rinse the pan and return the soup to it with the milk. Heat gently while preparing the croutons.

Toast the bread on one side only. Beat the butter or margarine with a little salt and pepper and the chopped parsley. Spread the mixture over the untoasted side of the bread and cook until lightly browned. Trim away the crusts if you wish, then cut the bread into tiny triangles or squares.

Season the soup to taste, then serve garnished with the croutons.

Butternut and Orange Soup

Serves 4–6

I first tasted this soup on vacation in South Africa. It is a wonderful combination of flavors and has quickly established itself as a family favorite. Do not boil the soup after adding the orange juice or the flavor will become slightly tainted.

1 onion, chopped
2 Tbsps vegetable oil
1–2 butternut squashes, weighing about
   2 pounds, peeled and diced
Grated rind and juice of 2 oranges
6 cups well-flavored vegetable broth
Salt and freshly ground black pepper
2 bay leaves
Freshly grated nutmeg
2 Tbsps freshly chopped parsley

Cook the onion in the oil until softened but not browned, then add the prepared squash and cook slowly for 5 minutes, stirring occasionally. Stir in the grated orange rind then add the broth, bay leaves, and seasonings. Bring the soup to a boil then cover and simmer for 40 minutes, until the squash is tender and cooked through.

Allow the soup to cool slightly, remove the bay leaves, then purée in a blender or food processor until smooth. Rinse the pan and return the soup to it, adding the orange juice. Reheat the soup slowly —do not let it boil—then season to taste. Add the freshly chopped parsley just before serving.

Butternut and Orange Soup ▶

Mexican Bean Soup

Serves 6

Pinto beans are the traditional beans for Mexican cookery, but they have been replaced in many dishes by red kidney beans, which are a more attractive color. If you are unable to get the pintos, use just kidney beans to make this thick and spicy soup.

½ cup red kidney beans, soaked overnight
½ cup pinto beans, soaked overnight
1 large onion, chopped finely
1 Tbsp oil
1 red chile, seeded and chopped finely
1 large clove garlic, sliced finely
1 tsp mild chile powder
1 Tbsp cilantro leaves
6 cups well-flavored vegetable broth
1 Tbsp tomato paste
Salt and freshly ground black pepper
½ cup Monterey Jack or Cheddar cheese, grated
Guacamole for serving

Drain the beans and rinse them thoroughly under cold running water, then set aside until needed. Cook the onion in the oil until soft, then add the chile, garlic, and chile powder and cook for another minute.

Stir the beans into the pan then add the cilantro, broth, tomato paste, and seasonings. Bring the soup to a boil and boil for 10 minutes, then simmer slowly for 45–60 minutes, until the beans are soft. Allow the soup to cool, then purée until smooth in a blender or food processor. Rinse the pan then return the soup to it and reheat gently, seasoning to taste with salt and pepper.

Scatter the cheese over the soup just before serving and set out a dish of guacamole.

◀ Mexican Bean Soup

Artichoke and Corn Soup

Serves 6

I love this soup, partly because it is such a good way of using up Jerusalem artichokes, which can become all-invasive in the garden! The flavor is sweet and creamy—a real winter warmer.

1 onion, chopped finely
1 oz butter
1 pound Jerusalem artichokes, washed and
    roughly chopped
2 cups frozen corn
4 cups well-flavored vegetable broth
Salt and freshly ground black pepper
2 tsps dried sweet bell pepper flakes (optional)
1 cup milk
3 Tbsps sour cream
Freshly chopped chives for garnish

Cook the onion in the butter until soft, then add the artichokes and corn. Stir the vegetables over the heat until the corn kernels start to defrost, then add the stock and seasonings and bring to a boil. Simmer the broth for 35–40 minutes, until the artichokes are tender.

Cool the soup slightly then purée until smooth in a blender or food processor. Rinse the pan and return the soup to it with the milk. Reheat gently, seasoning to taste, then stir in the sour cream and garnish with chopped chives just before serving.

Spinach and Zucchini Soup

Serves 8

This soup is a dramatic dark green in color and has a strong, peppery flavor.

   1 small onion, chopped finely
   1 Tbsp oil
   1–2 cloves garlic, crushed
   1 pound frozen leaf spinach
   2 zucchini, trimmed and grated
   6 cups well-flavored vegetable broth
   Salt and freshly ground black pepper
   Freshly grated nutmeg
   1 Tbsp fresh basil leaves, roughly torn
   Grated zucchini and whole-wheat croutons to
      garnish

Cook the onion in the oil until soft then add the garlic, spinach, and zucchini. Mix well, then stir in the broth and bring the soup to a boil. Season lightly with salt, pepper, and nutmeg then simmer the soup for 20 minutes.

Allow the soup to cool slightly, add the basil leaves, then purée until smooth in a blender or food processor. Rinse the pan and return the soup to it. Reheat gently, adding extra seasoning to taste, then serve the soup garnished with raw grated zucchini and whole-wheat croutons.

Minted Pea Soup

Serves 6

Pea Soup is one of the great classics. I always use frozen peas, because peas straight from the pod never make it as far as the saucepan! I add just a little lime for an extra brightness of flavor, but the essential ingredients are young peas and fresh mint. This soup is just as good hot or served cold over crushed ice in the summer.

   1 small onion, chopped finely
   1 oz butter
   1 pound frozen peas
   2 Tbsps freshly chopped mint
   5 cups water
   Grated rind of 1 lime
   Salt and white pepper to taste
   Light cream

Cook the onion slowly in the butter until soft but not brown; it is important to soften the onion really well as this soup has a very short cooking time. Stir in the peas and the mint, then add the water and bring the soup to a boil. Simmer for only 3 to 4 minutes, until the peas are just cooked —this will preserve the bright color of the soup.

Cool the soup slightly then add the lime rind and purée until smooth in a blender or food processor. Rinse the pan and return the soup to it, seasoning to taste with salt and white pepper. Reheat gently or allow to cool completely before chilling. Serve with a swirl of light cream.

Garbanzo Bean Soup with Red Pepper Salsa

Serves 6

Don't let the number of ingredients in this recipe put you off! It is a lightly spiced, creamy soup with a zingy salsa garnish—a real winner!

¾ cup garbanzo beans, soaked overnight
1 tsp cumin seeds
½ tsp mustard seeds, preferably white
1 Tbsp sesame seeds
1 large onion, sliced finely
1 Tbsp olive oil
2 large cloves garlic, sliced finely
½ tsp ground ginger
4 cups well-flavored broth
Salt and freshly ground black pepper
1 cup milk

Salsa
½ small red bell pepper, chopped
¼ cucumber, chopped
½ small red onion, chopped finely
1 clove garlic, chopped finely
1 tomato, chopped
1 small red chile, seeded and chopped finely
1–2 Tbsps cilantro leaves, finely torn
Grated rind and juice of 1 lemon
1–2 Tbsps sour cream (optional)

Drain the garbanzo beans and rinse them thoroughly under cold running water; set aside. Heat a nonstick skillet until evenly hot, then add the cumin, mustard, and sesame seeds and roast for 2 to 3 minutes, until they start to pop. Transfer the spices to a mortar or a spice mill and grind until smooth. You may also use the end of a rolling pin to grind the spices.

Cook the onion in the oil in a large pan until well browned, then add the garlic, ginger, and freshly ground spices and cook slowly for another minute. Stir in the garbanzo beans, and the broth, then bring the soup to a boil and season lightly. Simmer for 45–60 minutes, until the garbanzo beans are soft.

Prepare the salsa while the soup is cooking. Mix together all the prepared vegetables, season lightly, then add the cilantro, lemon rind, and lemon juice. Allow the salsa to stand for at least 30 minutes for the flavors to blend together.

Allow the soup to cool slightly, then purée until smooth in a blender or food processor. Rinse the pan and return the soup to it, then reheat gently with the milk, seasoning with salt and pepper to taste. Blend the salsa with 1 to 2 tablespoons of sour cream, if wished, then serve the soup with a generous spoonful of salsa in each portion.

▲ Garbanzo Bean Soup with Red Pepper Salsa

Mulligatawny Soup

Serves 4–6

There are many ways of serving Mulligatawny Soup, a classic eighteenth-century dish, but this is my favorite. Some people serve the rice and apple as separate garnishes, but I like to heat them through in the soup, especially if the rice is left over from another dish. Mulligatawny is from a Tamil word meaning "pepper water"; before chiles were widely available in Asia, all the heat in curries and other spicy dishes came from peppercorns.

2 onions, sliced finely
3 Tbsps vegetable oil
1 chicken (about 3 pounds) jointed and skinned
1–2 Tbsps mild curry powder, according to taste
½ tsp ground cloves
⅔ cup plain low fat yogurt
6 cups water
1 tsp salt
Freshly ground black pepper
1 cup cooked rice
1 tart red apple, cored and diced
Juice of ½ a lemon

Cook the onion in the oil until soft then add the chicken pieces. Continue to cook over moderate heat until browned all over. Add the curry powder and ground cloves and cook for a further 1 minute, then stir in the yogurt and heat until the yogurt has loosened any sediment from the bottom of the pan. Add the water to the pan with the salt and pepper, bring to a boil, then simmer, covered, for 1 hour, or until the chicken begins to fall off the bone.

Take the meat from the bone and return it to the pan with the cooked rice. Toss the apple in the lemon juice, add that to the pan, and return the soup to a boil. Simmer for 2 to 3 minutes, then season to taste and serve.

Minestrone

Serves 8

There are many recipes for this classic dish originating from different regions of Italy, each claiming to be the authentic soup. This version is thickened with both lentils and spaghetti and provides a hearty appetizer that is really a meal in itself.

1 large onion, chopped finely
1 leek, trimmed and sliced finely
4 strips bacon, diced finely
2 Tbsps olive oil
1 cup finely diced carrot
⅓ cup red lentils
2 14-oz cans chopped tomatoes
4 cups well-seasoned vegetable or chicken broth
Salt and freshly ground black pepper
2 Tbsps freshly chopped herbs
¾ cup shredded cabbage
½ cup broken whole-wheat spaghetti
2–3 Tbsps pesto sauce

Cook the onion, leek, and bacon in the oil until softened (but not browned), then stir in the carrot and cook for a further 1 to 2 minutes. Add the lentils, tomatoes, broth, herbs, and seasonings and bring to a boil, then cover the pan and simmer for 20 minutes.

Add the cabbage and spaghetti, return the soup to a boil, then simmer for a further 10 minutes. Season to taste, stir in the pesto, and serve immediately.

Broccoli Soup

Serves 6

It is hard to imagine a simpler soup than this, or one that is more delicious. The flavor of the broccoli is delicate, almost like asparagus, and I prefer to use water rather than broth to allow that flavor to shine through.

1 onion, chopped finely
1 Tbsp butter
2 large heads broccoli, weighing about 1 pound in total
Salt and freshly ground black pepper
4 cups water
2 cups milk
Freshly grated nutmeg to taste
Light cream (optional)

Cook the onion in the butter until softened but not browned. Trim the broccoli and chop it roughly, using the stalks and the florets. Add the broccoli to the pan, tossing it in the hot juices, then season lightly and add the water. Bring to a boil then simmer for 30–40 minutes, until the broccoli is soft.

Cool slightly, then purée the soup in a blender or food processor. Rinse the pan and return the soup to it with the milk, then heat slowly until almost at a boil. Remove from the heat; season to taste with salt, pepper, and nutmeg; then serve immediately with a swirl of cream.

◄ Minestrone

French Onion Soup

Serves 6

Believe it or not, this soup is the traditional French pick-me-up for the early morning after the night before! The flavor is supposed to galvanize you back into life.

soups and chowders

2 cups sliced onions
1 Tbsp butter
2 Tbsps olive oil
2 Tbsps fine whole-wheat flour
4 cups well flavored vegetable broth
Salt and freshly ground black pepper
3 bay leaves
4–6 slices whole-wheat French bread
½ cup grated Swiss cheese

Cook the onions in the butter and oil over high heat in a flame-proof casserole dish until softened and well browned; this may take up to 10 minutes. Stir the flour into the onions and cook gently for 1 to 2 minutes. Remove from heat and gradually add the broth to the pan, stirring all the time, then season lightly and add the bay leaves. Return the pan to the heat and bring the soup gradually to a boil, then cover and simmer for 45 minutes. The soup should be a rich, dark brown color.

Preheat a broiler. Remove the bay leaves and season the soup to taste. Drop the slices of bread into the soup, 1 per serving, then scatter the cheese over the bread. Cook under the hot broiler until the cheese has melted and is bubbling. Serve immediately, with 1 slice of bread in each portion.

French Onion Soup ▶

Chestnut and Blue Cheese Soup

Serves 6

A very rich soup. This is thick, smoky, and delicious. I use frozen chestnuts for convenience but dried, fresh, or canned chestnuts work just as well.

1 Tbsp vegetable oil
6–8 scallions, trimmed and chopped finely
4 strips bacon, chopped
1 pound peeled chestnuts, fresh, frozen, or canned; or 2 cups dried chestnuts, soaked overnight
4 cups vegetable broth
2 bay leaves
Salt and freshly ground black pepper
2 cups milk
¾ cup crumbled blue cheese, e.g., Danish or Stilton
Freshly chopped chives to garnish

Heat the oil in a pan, add the scallions and bacon and cook slowly until the scallions are soft. Add the chestnuts, broth, and bay leaves with a little salt and pepper. Bring the soup to a boil then cover and simmer for 30 minutes.

Remove the bay leaf, and allow the soup to cool slightly then purée until smooth in a blender or food processor. Rinse the pan and return the soup to it, then add the milk and return gradually to a boil. Season the soup to taste, then add the crumbled cheese just before serving. Garnish with chopped chives.

Fennel and Walnut Soup

Serves 4–6

An aniseed-flavored soup with the fine texture of chopped walnuts. This sophisticated soup makes an excellent dinner party appetizer. Reserve any celery leaves and fennel fronds for garnish.

1 onion, chopped finely
1 head fennel, trimmed and sliced
3 stalks celery, trimmed and sliced
2 Tbsps vegetable oil
1 plump clove garlic, sliced finely
2 bay leaves
5 ½ cups vegetable broth
salt and freshly ground black pepper
½ cup sour cream or plain yogurt
½ cup walnuts, chopped finely
Freshly chopped parsley mixed with fennel fronds
    and celery leaves to garnish

Cook the prepared vegetables slowly in the oil until soft but not browned. Add the garlic, bay leaves, and broth and bring the soup to a boil. Cover the pan and simmer for 30–40 minutes, until the vegetables are tender.

Cool the soup slightly and remove bay leaves. Then purée until smooth in a blender or food processor. Rinse the pan and return the soup to it. Reheat gently and season to taste with salt and pepper, then stir in the sour cream or yogurt. Add the walnuts just before serving and garnish with any reserved chopped fennel fronds and celery leaves mixed with parsley.

Cream of Cauliflower and Cumin Soup

Serves 6

This is deliciously light flavored soup, cooked for the minimum time so that there is plenty of texture despite it being blended. Serve with a salsa of curried vegetables if you wish, but I prefer the subtly spiced flavor of the cauliflower to dominate.

1 tsp cumin seeds
⅔ cup diced onion (1 medium onion, chopped
    finely)
1 Tbsp oil
5 cups roughly chopped cauliflower, florets and
    stalks
2 cups milk
3 cups vegetable stock
Salt and freshly ground black pepper

Heat a dry skillet until hot then add the cumin seeds and roast for 1–2 minutes. Cool slightly then grind to a fine powder in a pestle and mortar or with the end of a rolling pin.

Cook the onion slowly in the oil until soft but not browned, then add the ground cumin and cauliflower. Continue cooking slowly for 1–2 minutes, then add the milk, stock, and seasonings. Bring to a boil, then simmer for just 10 minutes. Cool slightly before blending in a blender or food processor until smooth. Rinse the pan, return the soup to it and reheat, seasoning to taste.

Gazpacho

Serves 8

This is the classic cold tomato soup of Spain. Some people add a vast selection of vegetables as garnish, but I prefer to add just 2 or 3 chopped vegetables of varying colors—it gets too complicated otherwise! The soup must be really well chilled.

½ cucumber, chopped roughly
1 green bell pepper, seeded
1 red onion, chopped finely
3 cloves garlic, crushed
⅔ cup fresh white bread crumbs
3 14-oz cans chopped tomatoes
Salt
¼ cup white wine vinegar
¼ cup fruity olive oil
1 cup water or vegetable broth
Sugar

Garnish

1 small green bell pepper, seeded and chopped finely
½ cucumber, seeded and chopped finely
1 small red onion, chopped finely

Crushed ice

Purée all the soup ingredients together in a blender or food processor, adding as much water or broth as necessary to make a thick, smooth, creamy soup. Season well, adding sugar to taste, then chill the soup with about 12 ice cubes. The soup will become slightly more liquid as the ice melts in it.

Prepare the garnishes for the soup and serve them in small bowls. Serve each helping of soup over half a cup of crushed ice. There is nothing worse than a warm gazpacho but, properly chilled, it is the epitome of a lazy summer lunch.

Irish Barley Soup

Serves 6

Leeks grew wild in Ireland for many centuries and they are still as much a part of the Irish diet as oats and barley. Combining pearl barley with leeks in this tasty soup makes a very traditional dish.

3 cups finely sliced leeks
2 Tbsps olive oil
¾ cup shredded spinach
⅓ cup pearl barley
6 cups well-flavored chicken or vegetable broth
Bouquet garni
Salt and freshly ground black pepper
2 bay leaves
¼ cup heavy cream (optional)

Cook the leeks in the oil until softened but not browned, then add the spinach and cook briefly until wilted. Add the barley, broth, and bouquet garni, then bring to a boil. Season lightly and add the bay leaves, then cover the pan and simmer for about 1½ hours, until the barley is tender.

Remove the bouquet garni and bay leaves. Season to taste then stir in the cream, if used, and serve immediately with fresh crusty bread.

◀ Irish Barley Soup

Beet Soup with Horseradish

Serves 6

If you think of a soup made with beets you immediately think of Borscht, the classic Russian soup. When made with cabbage and a rich beef broth, I find the classic recipes too heavy, so I created my own variation. I use cooked beets and combine them with white turnips and horseradish for a peppery soup. Ensure that the beets have not been dressed in vinegar.

1 onion, chopped finely
2 medium white turnips, diced
1 Tbsp vegetable oil
1 pound cooked beets, diced
6 cups well-flavored vegetable or beef broth
Salt and freshly ground black pepper
4 bay leaves
2 tsps grated horseradish
½ cup sour cream
1 Tbsp freshly chopped chives

Cook the onion and the turnip in the oil until softened but not browned, then add the beet and the broth and bring to a boil. Reduce the heat, add the seasonings, bay leaves, and 1 teaspoon horseradish, then cover and simmer for 30–40 minutes.

Allow the soup to cool slightly and remove bay leaves. Then purée until smooth in a blender or food processor. Rinse the pan and return the soup to it, then reheat the soup gently. Mix the remaining horseradish and the chives into the sour cream. Season the soup to taste then serve with a large dollop of the flavored cream in each portion.

soups and chowders

Oatmeal Soup

Serves 4

The Irish and the Scots both use oats extensively in their cooking. I am not certain where this recipe originated, but it is economical to make and suitable for both family suppers and lavish entertaining.

1 Tbsp margarine or butter
1 onion, chopped finely
1 clove garlic, crushed
⅓ cup rolled oats
2½ cups well-flavored vegetable broth
1 cup milk
Salt and freshly ground black pepper
1 Tbsp freshly chopped parsley
⅔ cup sour cream
Paprika

Melt the margarine or butter in a large pan. Add the onion and garlic and cook slowly until soft, then stir in the oats. Add the broth, bring to a boil then cover and simmer slowly for 30 minutes, stirring occasionally. Cool slightly.

Purée the soup until smooth in a blender or food processor, then add the milk and blend again. Rinse the pan and return the soup to it, then reheat gently until almost boiling. Season to taste with salt and pepper, then add the parsley and sour cream and serve immediately, garnished with a sprinkling of paprika.

Buckwheat and Mushroom Soup

Serves 6

Buckwheat has a strong, slightly sweet, and fragrantly nutty flavor. It is often the principal ingredient of simple rustic soups and stews, but in this more luxurious recipe, it blends with fresh and dried mushrooms to produce a very creamy soup. Only a little buckwheat is required to achieve a subtle flavoring.

½ cup dried cep mushrooms
½ cup sherry
1 Tbsp butter
1 Tbsp olive oil
1 onion, chopped finely
2 stalks celery, chopped finely
2 strips bacon, chopped finely
3 cups roughly chopped mushrooms
2 plump cloves garlic, sliced finely
¼ cup raw buckwheat groats
5 cups well-flavored vegetable broth
Salt and freshly ground black pepper
Freshly grated nutmeg
1 cup milk
Cream and paprika for garnish

Soak the ceps in the sherry for at least 30 minutes before starting the soup. Heat the butter and the oil together then add the onion, celery, and bacon and cook slowly for about 5 minutes, until the vegetables have softened but not browned. Add the chopped mushrooms and garlic and cook slowly for a further 2 to 3 minutes, until the juices start to run from the mushrooms. Add the ceps and the sherry, then stir in the buckwheat and pour in the broth.

Bring the soup slowly to a boil, stirring up any sediment from the bottom of the pan. Season lightly with salt, pepper, and nutmeg then cover the pan and simmer the soup for 40 minutes.

Allow the soup to cool slightly then purée until smooth in a blender or food processor. Rinse the pan and return the soup to it with the milk. Reheat gently then season to taste. Garnish with a swirl of cream and a little paprika before serving.

Crab and Corn Soup

Serves 6

This is a classic Chinese soup with a creamy, fragrant combination of flavors. Because it is not puréed in a blender before serving, I use creamed corn so that the soup is not too lumpy. Some people like to thicken this soup with cornstarch, but I find it is not necessary.

15-oz can creamed corn
8-oz can white crab meat
5 cups well-flavored fish, chicken, or vegetable broth
Salt and freshly ground black pepper
1 Tbsp soy sauce
2 eggs whites
Freshly chopped scallions

Bring the corn, crab meat, broth, seasoning, and soy sauce to a boil in a large pan, stirring to mix the corn and the crab evenly throughout the soup. Simmer for 10 minutes.

Whisk the egg whites into soft peaks, then stir carefully into the soup just before serving. Garnish with freshly chopped scallions.

◀ Crab and Corn Soup

Pumpkin and Carrot Soup

Serves 8-10

This is an excellent combination of flavors and makes a richly colored soup. Use lovage if you can find it—it has a peppery, slightly bitter taste and complements the blandness of an orange pumpkin well. If lovage is not available, use a mixture of flat-leafed parsley and oregano.

1 onion, chopped finely
1 Tbsp vegetable oil
1 pound carrots, sliced
1 pound pumpkin purée, fresh or canned
6 cups well-flavored vegetable broth
Salt and freshly ground black pepper
2 Tbsps freshly chopped lovage
2 cups milk
1 Tbsp butter or margarine
1 clove garlic, crushed
2 slices whole-wheat bread, toasted

Cook the onion in the oil until lightly browned, then add the carrots and cook gently until just softening. Stir in the pumpkin purée, then add the broth and bring to a boil, adding the seasonings and half the lovage. Cover and simmer slowly for 30–40 minutes, until the carrots are tender.

Allow the soup to cool slightly then purée until smooth in a blender or food processor. Rinse the pan and return the soup to it with the milk, reheating gently and adding extra seasoning, if required, to taste.

Beat the butter then add the remaining lovage and the garlic, then season lightly. Toast the bread then spread it lightly with the butter and cut into small squares or triangles. Drop the toasts into the soup just before serving.

Tomato, Orange, and Lentil Soup

Serves 4–6

Simple flavors combine to make a substantial warming soup. The advantage of using red lentils over other beans is that they do not require any soaking, so it is comparatively quick to make.

1 large onion, chopped finely
1 Tbsp vegetable oil
Grated rind and juice of one orange
½ cup red lentils
14-oz can chopped tomatoes
4 cups well-flavored vegetable broth
Salt and freshly ground black pepper
2 Tbsps fresh basil leaves

Cook the onion in the oil until soft then add the orange rind and lentils. Quickly stir in the chopped tomatoes then add the broth and a little seasoning. Bring the soup to a boil then simmer for 30 minutes, until the lentils are soft.

Allow the soup to cool slightly, add half the basil, then purée until smooth in a blender or food processor. Rinse the pan and return the soup to it, adding the orange juice and the remaining basil leaves, torn into small pieces. Heat the soup gently—do not allow it to boil after adding the orange juice or the flavor will be tainted. Season to taste then serve with chunks of crusty bread.

Chicken and Bean Soup

Serves 6

This is based on an Italian recipe for a tomato and bean soup. It is really a meal in itself when served with crusty bread. Only small portions should be served as an appetizer.

2 Tbsps olive oil
2 chicken thighs
1 large onion, chopped finely
1 green bell pepper, seeded and cut into strips
1 red chile, seeded and finely chopped
2 cloves garlic, crushed
1 Tbsp freshly chopped oregano
1 Tbsp freshly chopped flat-leafed parsley
14-oz can chopped tomatoes
2 Tbsps tomato paste
5 cups well-flavored chicken or vegetable broth
Salt and freshly ground black pepper
15-oz can borlotti beans or mixed legumes, drained and rinsed
Freshly chopped parsley and Parmesan cheese to garnish

Heat the oil in a large pan; add the chicken and brown all over. Remove the chicken from the pan with a slotted spoon and set aside. Stir the onion into the pan juices and cook until softened but not browned. Add the pepper, chile, and garlic with the herbs and stir well. Add the tomatoes, tomato paste, and broth then return the chicken to the pan, season lightly, and bring the soup to a boil. Cover and simmer for 40–50 minutes, until the chicken is cooked.

Remove the chicken from the pan and take the meat from the bones. Shred the chicken and return it to the pan with the beans. Return the soup to a boil, then simmer for 3 to 4 minutes to heat the beans thoroughly.

Season the soup to taste, then garnish with extra parsley. Slivers of Parmesan cheese may be sprinkled into the soup before serving.

Chicken and Bean Soup ▸

Squash Chowder

Serves 6

Use any hard-skinned squash for this chowder. Crown Prince is my favorite but acorn will work just as well, although a smoother-skinned squash will be easier to peel.

3 cups Crown Prince squash, diced finely
2 strips bacon, diced finely
2 Tbsps fruity olive oil
4–5 sprigs fresh thyme
2 bay leaves
4 cups well-flavored vegetable broth
Salt and freshly ground black pepper
1 cup white cabbage, finely shredded
2 oz creamed coconut, crumbled or diced
1 cup milk
1 large tomato, diced finely
1 cup frozen shrimp (optional)
1 Tbsp white wine vinegar
Freshly chopped parsley to garnish

Cook the squash and the bacon in the oil in a heavy pan for 6 to 8 minutes, stirring frequently, until the squash is beginning to soften. Add the herbs and broth, season lightly, then bring to a boil. Reduce the heat and simmer for 10 minutes, then add the cabbage and creamed coconut and continue cooking for a further 10–15 minutes.

Remove the thyme and bay leaves, then add the milk and the chopped tomato with the shrimp, if desired. Return the chowder to a boil and cook for a further 5 minutes. Season to taste then add the vinegar and parsley just before serving.

Smoked Haddock Chowder

Serves 6

Smoked haddock makes delicious chowders because the firm flesh of the fish stays in flakes and contrasts well with the texture of the vegetables.

2 cups milk
8 oz smoked haddock fillet, skinned
1 Tbsp butter
1 small onion, chopped finely
2 stalks celery, chopped finely
2 medium potatoes, diced
2 cups fish broth or water
1 cup frozen peas
1 cup frozen corn
Salt and freshly ground black pepper
2 Tbsps freshly chopped parsley

Heat the milk in a skillet until almost boiling, then add the haddock and poach for 4 to 5 minutes. Remove the haddock with a slotted spoon and reserve the milk.

Melt the butter in a separate pan, then add the onion and celery and cook slowly until soft. Stir in the diced potato, broth, and the reserved milk and bring to a boil. Reduce the heat and simmer the soup for 15 minutes, until the potato is tender.

Add the peas and corn kernels and return the soup to a boil. Flake the haddock and add it to the chowder, then continue to cook for a further 2 to 3 minutes, until the peas and corn are cooked and the fish is hot.

Season the chowder to taste and stir in half the parsley. Garnish with the remaining parsley.

◄ Squash Chowder

Thai Spiced Chicken Chowder

Serves 4

A spicy soup that is a meal in itself. Peel the outer skin from the lemon grass then flatten slightly with the blade of a knife before finely chopping.

1–2 Tbsps peanut or sunflower oil
2 small, boneless chicken breasts, skinned and shredded
2 tsps Thai 7-Spice seasoning
1 stick lemon grass, chopped finely
2 medium potatoes, diced
3 cups chicken or vegetable broth
2 cups milk
3–4 scallions, trimmed and sliced finely
1 cup frozen peas
1–2 Tbsps satay sauce or peanut butter
Salt and freshly ground black pepper
1–2 Tbsps heavy cream to garnish

Heat the oil in a large pan; add the chicken and 7-Spice and cook quickly until the chicken begins to brown. Stir in the lemon grass and potato, then add the liquids. Bring the chowder slowly to a boil, then cover and simmer for 20 minutes.

Stir the scallions into the chowder with the peas; return to a boil then continue cooking for a further 5 minutes.

Add the satay sauce or peanut butter to the chowder just before serving. Remove from heat and stir until melted. Season to taste then serve, garnished with a spoonful of cream if desired.

salads and appetizers

Many of the salads included in this section are suitable as a side dish or as a main course with hot potatoes or crusty bread. If you are planning to serve a salad as a main course you will usually need to double the quantities to serve the same number of people.

Salads have come a long way in the last few years and designer lettuces and other unusual salad leaves offer all sorts of presentation opportunities for both the home cook and the professional chef. While the appearance of a salad is very important, the selection of the ingredients, which should all be at the very peak of their ripeness, is paramount. It is impossible to make a good salad from limp lettuce, underripe tomatoes and a hard, tasteless strawberry added for a touch of sophistication. Some of the best salads are made from the simplest of ingredients, all packed with flavor. The Spinach Salad included here is an excellent example of a very simple dish but, when the spinach is young and the tomatoes sun-ripened, it cannot be beat.

I always like to use a well-flavored homemade dressing for my salads, usually made with a fruity extra virgin olive oil. I use sherry vinegar and a generous amount of mustard, balanced with sugar, salt, and pepper. Taste the dressing, then keep adding seasonings until it is right.

Appetizers should always be small and fairly light. They are simply a taste of what is to follow and should never be too filling or too heavy. An appetizer should always leave you wanting more. Do not serve a very heavily seasoned dish before a delicate main course, which may seem bland and dull in comparison, but try to pick dishes that will complement each other.

Brown Rice Salad with Fruits and Seeds

Serves 6

This salad is just as good hot or cold. I always toss rice and other grains in vinaigrette while it is hot, to allow it to absorb the flavor of the dressing. Try adding strawberries to the salad when they are in season. I like to serve this on a bed of crisp romaine lettuce leaves.

1½ cups brown rice
⅓ cup sunflower seeds
¼ cup sesame seeds
⅓ cup pumpkin seeds
6 scallions, trimmed and sliced
1 large mango, peeled and diced
⅓ cup dried cranberries

Dressing
Grated rind and juice of 1 lemon
2 Tbsps clear honey
4 Tbsps sunflower or peanut oil
1 Tbsp dill weed, chopped roughly
Salt and freshly ground black pepper

Bring the rice to a boil in a large pan of cold water, then simmer for 20–25 minutes until just tender but not soggy.

Prepare the dressing while the rice is cooking. Whisk together all the ingredients, seasoning to taste with salt and pepper. Drain the rice, shake gently, then transfer it to a large bowl and add the dressing. Toss well, then leave until the rice has cooled, tossing from time to time.

Toast the sunflower seeds in a dry skillet for 2 to 3 minutes until they begin to brown, then add the sesame seeds and cook for a further 1 to 2 minutes. Allow to cool, then add to the pumpkin seeds.

Toss the cooled rice with the seeds, scallions, and fruits. Add a little extra seasoning if necessary and garnish with more dill just before serving.

Buckwheat Salad

Serves 6–8

Buckwheat is used extensively in eastern European cookery. It has a slightly sweet flavor; I prefer to use roasted groats for this recipe, as they are slightly nuttier. This is a very simple salad.

1 cup buckwheat groats, roasted or raw
3 cups well-flavored vegetable broth
3 Tbsps vinaigrette
1 cup diced carrot
½ cup diced cucumber
⅓ cup diced pickles
⅓ cup poppyseeds
⅓ cup freshly chopped parsley (optional)
Salt and freshly ground black pepper

Bring the buckwheat and broth to a boil then cover the pan and simmer for 30–35 minutes, until the broth has been absorbed and the groats are tender. Stir in the vinaigrette, then leave to cool completely.

Add all the remaining ingredients to the buckwheat and mix well, seasoning to taste. Serve the salad at room temperature.

Pear and Grape Salad

Serves 4

A delicious combination of tastes and textures. This salad makes an equally good appetizer or side dish to main dishes based on grains or beans.

2 Little Gem lettuces, or ½ head iceberg lettuce, torn into bite-sized pieces
1 head endive, trimmed and sliced
2 large ripe dessert pears, peeled and sliced
Juice of ½ a lemon
2 cups table grapes, preferably black, halved and seeded
½ cup sour cream
⅓ cup lowfat cream cheese
1–2 cloves garlic, crushed
Salt and freshly ground black pepper
Paprika

Mix together the lettuce and endive and arrange in a salad bowl or on individual plates. Toss the pears in the lemon juice and arrange the pieces over the lettuce, then add the grapes.

Blend together the sour cream and cream cheese, add the garlic, and season well with salt and pepper. Spoon the dressing into the center of the salad, garnish with paprika, then serve with fresh, crusty whole-wheat bread.

◀ Pear and Grape Salad

Pasta Salad

Serves 12 as an appetizer, 6–8 as a main course

Pasta salad makes an excellent buffet dish but, for everyday eating, it is a meal in itself. Some salads are dressed in vinaigrette, but I add strained cottage cheese or plain yogurt to a little mayonnaise. It complements the pasta much better. You may use white pasta if you prefer, as there is plenty of fiber in this salad from just the vegetables and beans.

8 oz whole-wheat pasta shapes of your choice
1 red bell pepper, seeded and diced
1½ cups button mushrooms, halved
1 cup diced cucumber
1½ cups corn kernels
6 scallions, sliced finely
15-oz can red kidney beans, drained and rinsed
1 cup diced Swiss cheese
Salt and freshly ground black pepper

Dressing

1½ cups strained cottage cheese or plain yogurt
1 cup mayonnaise
Salt and freshly ground black pepper
2–3 cloves garlic, crushed
⅓ cup freshly chopped chives

Salad leaves for serving

Bring a large pan of salted water to a boil and add the pasta. Return to a boil, then simmer as directed until just tender. Drain the pasta and rinse it in cold water, then let cool completely.

Mix all the prepared vegetables together and season lightly with salt and pepper. Blend all the ingredients for the dressing and season to taste.

Place the pasta in a large bowl, then top with the vegetables. Spoon on the dressing. If the salad is prepared in advance, I suggest leaving it in layers and tossing at the last minute. If it is to be served immediately, however, toss all the ingredients together then transfer the salad to a large platter, lined with greens.

Crunchy Corn Salad

Serves 4

Toasted sesame seeds, honey, and ginger in the dressing give an unusual sweetness to a colorful selection of crisp vegetables. Blanch the bean sprouts for one minute before adding them to the salad, if you prefer.

4 oz baby corn
4 oz snow peas, topped, tailed, and shredded
1 medium zucchini, trimmed and cut into matchsticks
1 large carrot, cut into matchsticks
1 cup bean sprouts
2 Tbsps sesame seeds, toasted

Dressing
2 Tbsps clear honey
1 Tbsp sesame oil
Grated rind and juice of 1 lime
2 pieces preserved stem ginger
2 Tbsps ginger syrup
2 Tbsps light soy sauce

Blanch the corn in a large pan of water for 2 minutes, then add the snow peas and cook for another minute. Drain the vegetables then plunge them immediately into cold water. Drain again when cold.

Combine the blanched vegetables with the carrot and zucchini sticks and the bean sprouts, then add the toasted sesame seeds.

Whisk together all the ingredients for the dressing and season to taste with salt and pepper. Pour the dressing over the salad vegetables and toss thoroughly before serving.

Apricot, Almond, and Tomato Salad

Serves 4-6

Served with warm crusty bread, this salad is a meal in itself. It also pairs perfectly with Curried Vegetable Casserole (see Main Dishes, pages 94–141).

¾ cup blanched almonds
Salt
Ground cayenne pepper
Salad leaves
4 ripe tomatoes, cut into wedges
1 cup dried apricots, chopped roughly
6 Tbsps mustard-flavored vinaigrette
Parsley

Heat a skillet, preferably nonstick, until evenly hot, then add the almonds. Cook over moderate heat until evenly browned on both sides (the almonds may be toasted if preferred). Dust some paper towels with salt and cayenne pepper, then add the hot almonds and toss until well coated with the seasonings. Allow to cool, tossing from time to time.

Line a salad bowl with mixed leaves of your choice. Mix together the tomatoes, chopped apricots, and deviled almonds and arrange them over the salad leaves. Spoon on the mustard vinaigrette and garnish with a sprig of parsley.

Apricot, Almond, and Tomato Salad ▶

Summer Couscous Salad

Serves 6

I often serve couscous cold as a salad, with just toasted pine nuts and a fruity olive oil dressing. This is more of a mixed vegetable salad, spiced with roasted peppers and chiles.

2 red bell peppers
3–4 chiles, according to taste
2 cups couscous
⅔ cup pine nuts, toasted
1 cup finely sliced button mushrooms
1 small zucchini, chopped finely
3 Tbsps vinaigrette or extra virgin olive oil
Salt and freshly ground black pepper
1 Tbsp freshly chopped parsley
1 avocado, sliced and tossed in lemon juice

Preheat oven to 400°F. Place the bell peppers and the chiles on a baking sheet and roast in the oven for 30–40 minutes, turning once during cooking. The chiles may only take 20 minutes to blacken and should be removed as soon as they are ready. Cover the hot peppers with a damp dish towel and leave until cool. Remove the skins by peeling from the flower end, then discard the core and seeds and chop the flesh.

Cover the couscous with boiling water and allow it to stand for at least 20 minutes; add a little more water if it seems dry, but do not drown the grains. Add the roasted peppers and all the remaining ingredients and toss thoroughly. Transfer to a bowl or platter and garnish with the avocado just before serving.

Date and Cottage Cheese Salad

Serves 4

I used to have a real thing about cottage cheese, refusing to eat it at all! Now I realize that it does mix well with other ingredients, providing you add strongly contrasting textures. The advantage of cottage cheese is that it is low in fat, whereas most other cheeses have a high fat content.

1 cup lowfat cottage cheese
½ cup pitted dates, chopped roughly
2 firm dessert pears
Juice of 1 lemon
2 oranges
2 heads endive, trimmed and sliced
Salt and freshly ground black pepper
Watercress or arugula leaves

Place the cottage cheese in a bowl and add the dates. Core and dice the pears, then toss them in the lemon juice. Peel the oranges and cut the rind into thin strips for garnish. Remove any seeds, then roughly chop the oranges. Add the pears to the cottage cheese with the oranges, and endive. Season the salad to taste with salt and pepper.

Line a suitable bowl or platter with watercress or arugula leaves, then pile the salad in the middle. Garnish with the reserved orange rind before serving.

◄ Summer Couscous Salad

Green and White Salad

Serves 6-8

This makes a welcome alternative to tabbouleh, the internationally renowned cracked wheat salad. The vegetables must be finely chopped or sliced so that there is not too much contrast between them and the wheat—the seeds provide all the contrast required.

1 cup cracked wheat
2 cups boiling water
⅓ cup pumpkin seeds
1 green bell pepper, seeded and chopped finely
2 stalks celery, sliced finely
1 small leek, trimmed and sliced finely
½ cucumber, diced finely
1 cup freshly chopped parsley
⅓ cup freshly chopped mixed herbs

Dressing
Grated rind and juice of 1 lime
¼ cup fruity extra virgin olive oil
Salt and freshly ground black pepper

Place the wheat in a bowl, pour the boiling water over, and leave for at least 30 minutes. Drain the wheat in a sieve then wring excess water out in a clean dish towel.

Place the wheat in a bowl with the seeds and prepared vegetables. The wheat and vegetables may be tossed together at the table, if you wish. Season lightly.

Whisk the dressing until blended then pour it through the salad. Top with a layer of the freshly chopped herbs, all mixed together. Toss all the ingredients just before serving.

Potato Niçoise

Serves 6–8

A salad Niçoise usually features tuna as its main ingredient. In this salad, I have used new potatoes—freshly cooked and still warm in their skins—for making a filling and satisfying main course salad. These quantities would also serve 4 as a main course.

1 pound small new potatoes, scrubbed
Salad greens
4 tomatoes, cut into wedges
¾ cup cold cooked fava beans
4 hard-boiled eggs, quartered
2 Tbsps freshly chopped mixed herbs
½ cup small black olives
Salt and freshly ground black pepper
2-oz can anchovy fillets
2 Tbsps butter

Bring the potatoes to a boil in a pan of water, then simmer for 10–12 minutes, or until just cooked.

Prepare the salad while the potatoes are cooking. Cover the bottom of a large bowl or platter with the greens, then arrange the tomatoes, fava beans and hard-boiled eggs around the edge. Sprinkle the salad with the herbs and olives, then season lightly with salt and pepper. Cut the anchovy fillets in half lengthwise and arrange the pieces over the salad, reserving the oil.
Drain the potatoes and return them to the pan. Add the butter, tossing the potatoes until it has melted, then pile the potatoes into the center of the salad. Add the oil from the anchovies to the butter left in the pan, stir in a few grinds of pepper, then pour the mixture over the salad and serve immediately.

Cucumber Tabbouleh

Serves 6

A traditional tabbouleh is almost green in color from the high proportion of herbs to cracked wheat. It is important to dry the wheat thoroughly or the finished salad will be soggy and unpalatable.

1 cup fine cracked wheat or bulgur
2 cups boiling water
⅓ cup freshly chopped parsley
⅓ cup freshly chopped mint
2 tomatoes, seeded and chopped
2 scallions, trimmed and chopped finely
1⅓ cups diced cucumber
Juice of 1 lime
Salt and freshly ground black pepper
¼ cup fruity olive oil

Allow the cracked wheat to soak in the boiling water for 30 minutes then drain, if necessary, and squeeze dry in a clean dish towel.

Place the wheat in a large bowl and add all the remaining ingredients, including seasonings to taste. Toss the salad well and serve at room temperature.

Eggplant Pâté

Serves 6–8

I always think of this as a pâté although it is soft enough to be used as a dip. It oozes Mediterranean promise and should certainly be included in any summer buffet.

1 onion, chopped finely
1 Tbsp olive oil
1 medium eggplant, trimmed and sliced thinly
1 clove garlic, crushed
½ cup thick tomato juice
1 Tbsp fresh oregano leaves
1 cup low-fat cream cheese
Salt and freshly ground black pepper

Cook the onion in the oil until it starts to soften, then add the eggplant slices and cook, covered, for about 10 minutes until tender. Add the garlic and allow to cool.

Blend the eggplant mixture with all the remaining ingredients in a blender or food processor until almost smooth - I always find the eggplant skin keeps the texture of the pâté slightly grainy. Season to taste, then chill for 30 minutes. The pâté should not be served too cold as this will inhibit the flavor—if it has been chilled overnight it should be allowed to stand at room temperature for about an hour before serving.

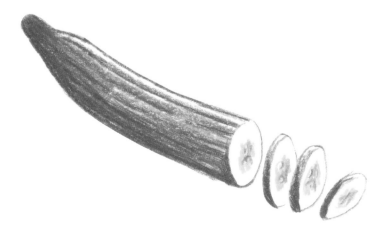

◀ Cucumber Tabbouleh

Crab with Ginger and Grapefruit

Serves 2

I first had this dish in a restaurant near Selsey, one of the best crab producing areas in England. The freshness of the ginger and grapefruit cut through the richness of the crab as well as adding fiber, making it a well-balanced and substantial starter.

2 dressed crabs
½ cup fresh brown bread crumbs
1 grapefruit
Salt and freshly ground black pepper
1 inch fresh ginger root, coarsely grated

Scoop the crabmeat from the shells into a bowl and mix it with the bread crumbs. Grate the rind from the grapefruit, then add it to the crab with the chopped flesh of the fruit. Season well, then add the ginger. Pile the mixture back into the shells and carefully clean the edges.

Preheat a broiler, then cook the crabs under a medium heat for 5–6 minutes until piping hot. Serve just as they are, or with a very small salad garnish.

Beet and Sorrel Salad

Serves 4

This is a simple salad of robust flavors. Do not add the beet until just before serving, to prevent the color from "bleeding" into the other ingredients.

Salad greens
3 oz watercress, trimmed, washed, and shaken dry
1 cup young sorrel leaves, shredded roughly
1 cup shredded celeriac
Grated rind and juice of 1 lemon
4 small beets, cooked and diced

Dressing
4 Tbsps fruity olive oil
1 Tbsp sherry vinegar
½ tsp sugar
1 Tbsp Dijon or yellow mustard
Salt and freshly ground black pepper

Arrange the salad greens in a bowl or on a platter, then add the watercress and sorrel and mix well. Toss the celeriac with the lemon rind and juice and add to the salad with the diced beet.

Whisk all the ingredients for the dressing together; the mustard will make the dressing quite thick. Pour over the salad, toss, then serve immediately.

Spinach Salad

Serves 4

This is one of my favorite salads—it is packed with really pungent flavors, guaranteed to titillate the most jaded of palates. The quantities are a rough guide only—vary the amounts according to the number of diners and their appetites. The salad should be dressed at the last moment and completely eaten up once made.

⅓ cup pine nuts
4 handfuls young spinach leaves, washed and dried
2 handfuls arugula, loosely packed
1 cup cherry tomatoes, halved
Shavings of fresh Parmesan cheese
Salt and freshly ground black pepper
4–5 Tbsps garlic vinaigrette dressing

Heat a nonstick skillet until evenly hot; add the pine nuts and cook until golden brown on both sides, shaking the pan almost continuously. Allow the nuts to cool on paper towels.

Mix the spinach and arugula together in a large, flat dish, tearing the arugula into bite-sized pieces. Add the tomatoes and pine nuts, then add Parmesan cheese to taste; an easy way to cut the shavings is with a potato peeler.

Season the salad lightly with salt and pepper, then add the vinaigrette and toss before serving.

Roasted Endive and Pink Grapefruit Salad

Serves 4

I love endive but I prefer it cooked to raw. This salad combines roasted endive which is still quite crisp with tomatoes and the exciting zing of grapefruit.

2 heads endive, trimmed
1 Tbsp finely chopped onion
Salt and freshly ground black pepper
1 Tbsp olive oil
⅓ cup pine kernels
2 tomatoes, halved and sliced
1 ruby grapefruit, cut into segments
1–2 Tbsps freshly chopped chives
Salt and freshly ground black pepper
1–2 Tbsps fruity olive oil

Preheat oven to 425°F. Cut the endive in half lengthways and place in a roasting tin. Scatter the onion over, season well and drizzle with the oil. Roast in the preheated oven for 15 minutes, then allow to cool.

Toast the pine kernels in a hot dry skillet for 3–4 minutes until browned then allow to cool.

Slice the roasted endive and mix it with the pine kernels, tomatoes, grapefruit, and chives. Season well, spoon the olive oil over then serve the salad on a bed of lettuce or raw spinach.

Waldorf Salad

Serves 6-8

I often teach children's cooking courses in the summer and this is one of the salads we make for the parents' lunch at the end of the course. Mixing yogurt with mayonnaise makes a much milder dressing for the salad.

2 crisp, sweet red apples, cored and diced
2 tart green apples, cored and diced
Juice of 1 lemon
1 head celery, trimmed and sliced
2 cups walnut pieces, roughly chopped
Salt and freshly ground black pepper
1 cup thick plain yogurt
½ cup mayonnaise
Lettuce leaves
Paprika

Toss the diced apples in the lemon juice to prevent them from browning. Mix the apples with the celery and walnuts and season well.

Blend the yogurt and mayonnaise together then spoon over the salad. Toss until all the ingredients are evenly coated; add extra mayonnaise if necessary.

Line a bowl with lettuce leaves, then pile the salad into the bowl. Sprinkle a little paprika over the salad just before serving.

Lentil Salad

Serves 4–6

Sometimes salads need inspiration. This mixture of curried vegetables makes an excellent and filling winter salad.

15-oz can green lentils, drained and rinsed, or
  ¾ cup freshly cooked lentils
1 cup grated carrot
2 stalks celery, chopped finely
⅓ cup golden raisins
1 Tbsp freshly chopped cilantro

Dressing
3 Tbsps sunflower oil
1 Tbsp white wine vinegar
½ tsp curry powder
Salt and freshly ground black pepper

Combine all the salad ingredients in a bowl. Whisk together the oil and vinegar for the dressing, add the curry powder, then season to taste. Pour the dressing into the bowl, toss the salad well, then chill lightly for about 30 minutes before serving.

Rice and Pistachio Salad

Serves 4–6

Wild rice is available either by itself or in a mix with instant white rice. The latter makes an ideal base for this salad, which is mixed with raisins and pistachios and thickened with a honey dressing.

1½ cups wild and white rice mix
½ cup raisins
½ cup pistachios, shelled
4 scallions, trimmed and sliced
4 tomatoes, chopped

Dressing
¼ cup clear honey
1 Tbsp cider vinegar
Grated rind and juice of 1 lemon
2 Tbsps olive oil
Salt and freshly ground black pepper
1 Tbsp freshly chopped chives

Bring the rices to a boil in plenty of water, then cover and simmer for 20 minutes. While the rice is cooking, whisk all the ingredients for the dressing together and season to taste. Drain the rice thoroughly then add the dressing and toss it with the grains. Transfer the rice to a bowl and allow it to cool completely.

Add the remaining ingredients to the salad and stir them carefully into the rice. Season to taste with extra salt and pepper before serving.

Flageolet and Tuna Salad

Serves 3–4

I always keep a can of flageolet beans in my pantry because they make such excellent salads. This idea is based on an Italian antipasto. The beans make a small amount of tuna go a very long way.

15-oz can flageolet beans, drained and rinsed
3½-ounce can tuna
1 small red onion, sliced finely
1–2 cloves garlic, sliced finely
2 ripe tomatoes, seeded and chopped
1 Tbsp capers
Salt and freshly ground black pepper
3 Tbsps olive oil
Small romaine lettuce leaves

Place the beans in a bowl. Drain and flake the tuna, then add it to the beans with the onion, garlic, tomatoes, and capers. Stir in seasoning to taste, then moisten the salad with the oil.

Arrange some romaine leaves on a serving platter and pile the salad in middle. Wedges of hard-boiled egg may be added if desired.

Rice and Pistachio Salad ▶

Mushroom and Hazelnut Pâté

Serves 6–8

A flavorful vegetarian pâté that slices well. I serve two thin slices per person, propped up on a small mound of dressed salad leaves.

   1½ cups hazelnuts, toasted and roughly chopped
   1½ cups fresh whole-wheat bread crumbs, tightly packed
   1 medium onion
   2 plump cloves garlic
   1 pound mushrooms, trimmed
   4 Tbsps butter
   Salt and freshly ground black pepper
   2 Tbsps soy sauce
   1 large egg, beaten
   2 thin strips bacon (optional)

Preheat oven to 350°F. Combine the hazelnuts with the bread crumbs in a bowl. Chop the onion, garlic, and mushrooms finely—this is best done in a food processor.

Melt the butter in a large skillet, add the mushroom mixture, and cook slowly for about 5 minutes, until the juices run from the mushrooms. Allow to cool slightly, then add to the hazelnut mixture with plenty of salt, pepper, and the soy sauce. Blend together with the beaten egg.

Lightly grease a small loaf pan. Stretch the bacon with the back of a knife, then arrange it in the base of the pan. Spoon the hazelnut mixture into the pan and smooth the top. Cover with greased foil and place in a shallow roasting pan. Half fill the roasting pan with hot water.

Bake in the preheated oven for 1 hour, then remove the pâté from the roasting pan and allow to cool. Chill the pâté overnight in the refrigerator, then loosen it in the pan with a flat knife. Turn out onto a serving plate and serve on a bed of greens.

◀ Mushroom and Hazelnut Pâté

Deviled Leek Crostini

Serves 4

These delicious toasts may be served with a crisp salad or with soup. If preferred, the topping may be spread over crackers or French toasts for baking, but commercial crackers may become soft on heating.

   4 slices whole-wheat or light whole-wheat bread
   2 leeks, sliced finely
   2 plump cloves garlic, crushed
   3 Tbsps fruity olive oil
   1 tsp dry mustard powder, or 2 tsps mustard
   1 tsp cayenne pepper
   ⅔ cup freshly grated Parmesan cheese
   3 Tbsps sour cream

Preheat oven to 350°F. Bake the bread on a baking sheet for 25–30 minutes, until dry and crisp. The bread may be brushed lightly with olive oil before baking for extra flavor.

Cook the leeks and garlic in the oil until they begin to soften, then add the mustard and cayenne. Continue cooking until the leeks are very soft. Add the cheese and cream then season well with salt, pepper, and extra cayenne as required.

Spread the leeks over the prepared toasts and cook under a hot broiler for 2 to 3 minutes, until the leeks start to brown. Serve immediately.

Warm Jalapeno Bean Dip

Serves 8

Refried beans—mashed pinto beans—are a staple of the Mexican diet and are often served as a side dish with tacos and burritos. This dip is made with canned beans for convenience. Serve it warm as part of a Mexican meal or appetizer as well as cold as a dip.

4 scallions, chopped finely
1 jalapeno chile, seeded and chopped finely
1 clove garlic, crushed
1 Tbsp olive oil
16 oz refried beans
1 Tbsp freshly chopped cilantro
2 tomatoes, chopped finely
⅔ cup sour cream
Salt

Cook the scallions, chile, and garlic in the oil until softened but not browned. Add the refried beans and heat gently for 2 or 3 minutes before adding the cilantro, tomatoes, and sour cream. Mix carefully and continue heating gently for a further 2 or 3 minutes. Season to taste with salt then serve immediately with tortilla chips, sliced vegetables, or flat breads.

Roasted Tomato Tartlets

Serves 6

This is a wonderful dish to make when home-grown tomatoes are plentiful and full of flavor. Add a few olives to the filling if you wish - they look attractive, but if the tomatoes are ripe and flavorful, they are not necessary.

Dough
1½ cups fine whole-wheat flour
¼ cup sesame seeds
½ tsp salt
1 large egg, beaten
⅓ cup olive oil
3–4 Tbsps water

3 onions, sliced finely
2 cloves garlic, halved
3 Tbsps fruity olive oil
3–4 sprigs fresh thyme
2 bay leaves
4–5 large tomatoes, sliced
Salt and freshly ground black pepper

Mix together the flour, sesame seeds, and salt, then make a well in the center. Add the egg and olive oil and mix to a soft dough, adding water as necessary. Divide the mixture into six and shape to line 6 4-inch individual tart tins—this is more of a dough than a pastry and is easiest to mold into shape with your fingers. Chill the tart shells for at least 30 minutes while preparing the filling.

Cook the onions and garlic in the olive oil with the thyme and bay leaves for 30–40 minutes, until well softened and reduced. Season to taste with salt and pepper, then remove the herbs.

Preheat an oven to 425°F. Fill the tart shells with the onion mixture then top with the tomatoes, overlapping the slices and brushing them lightly with olive oil. Season well with salt and pepper, then bake in the preheated oven for 20–25 minutes, until the dough is crisp and the tomatoes are just starting to blacken. Serve hot or cold with a small, leafy salad.

Roasted Tomato Tartlets ▶

Stuffed Zucchini with Tomato Sauce

Serves 4

I like to serve a warm appetizer, especially in the winter—it sets the scene and indicates that you have gone to some trouble over the meal! A stuffed vegetable always looks good and zucchini are the perfect boat-shaped holders for any number of fillings.

- 4 small zucchini, trimmed
- 1 large onion, chopped finely
- 1 cup roughly chopped button mushrooms
- 2 cloves garlic
- 2 Tbsps oil
- ½ cup fresh whole-wheat bread crumbs
- Salt and freshly ground black pepper
- 1 Tbsp pine nuts
- 1 Tbsp sunflower seeds
- 1 Tbsp fresh basil leaves, roughly torn
- 14-oz can chopped tomatoes
- ½ cup grated Cheddar cheese (optional)

Preheat oven to 375°F. Cut each zucchini in half lengthwise and scoop out the flesh with a teaspoon. Arrange the shells in a buttered ovenproof dish, chop the reserved flesh, and set to one side.

Finely chop half the onion, the mushrooms, and 1 clove of garlic in a food processor. Cook the mixture in 1 tablespoon of oil until the juices run from the mushrooms, then remove from the heat and mix in the bread crumbs, seasonings, and zucchini flesh. Add the pine nuts and sunflower seeds, then stuff the mixture into the zucchini shells, and pack well.

Prepare the tomato sauce by cooking the remaining onion in the remaining oil until soft. Crush the remaining garlic and add it with the tomatoes and basil. Season well, then simmer for about 10 minutes, until reduced and thickened. Pour the sauce over the stuffed zucchini, sprinkle with the grated cheese if used, then bake in the preheated oven for 20–25 minutes, until the vegetable shells are tender. Serve with a salad.

◀ Stuffed Zucchini with Tomato Sauce

Quick-Bake Calabrian Pizzas

Serves 6

These pizzas are full of the zesty flavors of southern Italy—strong, pungent, and exciting. Serve as an appetizer or main dish or as cocktail nibbles, cut into wedges and served warm.

Dough
- 2 cups whole-wheat flour
- 1 tsp salt
- 1 package active dry yeast
- 1 Tbsp olive oil
- ¾ cup warm water

- 6 tsps tapenade
- 1 onion, sliced finely
- 12 halves sun-dried tomatoes in oil, chopped
- 1 Tbsp basil leaves, roughly torn
- Salt and freshly ground black pepper
- 2-oz can anchovy fillets, chopped
- 4 oz mozzarella cheese, sliced

Mix together the flour, salt, and yeast in a bowl and make a well in the center. Add the oil and most of the water, then mix to a soft but manageable dough, adding more water if necessary. Knead well until smooth and elastic.

Preheat the oven to 425°F. Divide the dough into 6 parts and roll out into circles 6-inches in diameter. Fold the edges of the dough over to form a lip, then place the bases on lightly greased baking sheets. Cover and leave in a warm place for 20–25 minutes, until the dough rises.

Spread each pizza base with 1 teaspoon of tapenade, then arrange the onion over the bases and scatter with the chopped sun-dried tomatoes. Add the torn basil leaves with plenty of salt and pepper, then scatter the chopped anchovies over the pizzas. Arrange the mozzarella slices over the pizzas then spoon the oil from the anchovies over the cheese.

Bake the pizzas in the preheated oven for 15 minutes, until the bases are crisp and the cheese has melted. Serve immediately.

Spiced Vegetables with Yogurt

Serves 6

A good appetizer to serve before a mildly flavored main course, this dish combines a variety of typical curry vegetables with garbanzo beans and a tangy yogurt dressing. It may be served cold, but I prefer it warm. Do not reheat the dish after adding the yogurt, as it is likely to separate and become watery.

salads and appetizers

4 cups prepared vegetables (zucchini, eggplant, bell pepper, cucumber, onions, mushrooms, etc.) sliced or cut into matchsticks
2 plump cloves garlic, crushed
1 tsp cumin seeds
1 Tbsp coriander seeds
3 green cardamoms, crushed and seeded
3 Tbsps oil
¾ cup garbanzo beans, freshly cooked or canned
1 cup thick plain yogurt
Grated rind of 1 lemon
2 Tbsps freshly chopped cilantro
Salt and freshly ground black pepper
1 Tbsp finely grated fresh gingerroot
Crusty or flat breads

Prepare the vegetables and mix with the crushed garlic. Heat a nonstick skillet and add the cumin, coriander, and cardamom seeds. Fry gently for 1 to 2 minutes until the seeds begin to pop, then transfer the spices to a mortar and pestle or a spice mill and grind—the ground spices may be sifted to remove excess coriander husks, if preferred.

Heat the oil in the spice pan, add the vegetables, and cook for 4 to 5 minutes, until they begin to soften. Return the spices to the pan, add the garbanzo beans, and continue cooking until the vegetables are just tender and the beans are hot.

Mix the yogurt with the lemon rind and chopped cilantro, then pour it over the vegetables in the pan. Mix gently then add salt and pepper to taste before adding the grated ginger. Serve immediately, or let cool first.

Ratatouille with Melon

Serves 8

I first tasted a ratatouille with melon on vacation in South Africa—it was stunning. I like to use Galia or Cantaloupe melon as I find they contrast well, both in flavor and texture, with the traditional ratatouille ingredients. Watermelon is a good alternative.

1 large onion, sliced
1 medium eggplant, sliced
4 Tbsps olive oil
2 zucchini, sliced thickly
1 green bell pepper, diced
2–3 plump cloves garlic, sliced finely
2 14-oz cans chopped tomatoes
Salt and freshly ground black pepper
2–3 Tbsps freshly torn basil leaves
2–3 cups melon balls, either Galia, Cantaloupe,
   or watermelon

Cook the onion and eggplant in the olive oil until the eggplant starts to brown, then add the zucchini, bell pepper, and garlic and cook for a further 5 minutes. Add the chopped tomatoes, salt, and pepper and bring to a boil. Simmer for about 10 minutes, until the sauce has thickened but the vegetables still retain their texture.

Season the ratatouille to taste then leave to cool. Add the basil and melon just before serving at room temperature.

◄ Ratatouille with Melon

Hummus

Serves 8

This garbanzo bean dip originates in the Middle East and may be eaten with breads or sliced fresh vegetables. Many people blend it with just olive oil, but I often find this too greasy. I recommend keeping back some of the cooking water from the beans to make the purée.

  1 cup garbanzo beans, soaked overnight
  2–3 plump cloves garlic
  ½ cup tahini
  ⅓ cup olive oil
  Salt and freshly ground black pepper
  Juice of ½ a lemon (optional)
  Paprika

Rinse the garbanzo beans under cold running water, then bring them to a boil in a pan of fresh water and simmer for about 1½ hours, until tender. Leave to cool, then drain the beans, reserving some of the water.

Place the garbanzo beans in a blender or food processor with the garlic, tahini, and olive oil and blend. Add as much water from the beans as necessary to make a thick paste—about ⅔ cup. Season well with salt and pepper, then add lemon juice to taste.

Spoon the hummus into a serving dish and chill lightly. Sprinkle with paprika just before serving.

Guacamole

Serves 4

If you think you can make satisfactory guacamole by adding water to a mix, think again! A true guacamole should be slightly rough in texture, not blended to a uniformly smooth paste.

  2 large ripe avocados
  2 tomatoes, seeded and chopped
  1 mild green chile, seeded and chopped finely
  Grated rind and juice of 1 lime
  2 scallions, trimmed and chopped finely
  1–2 cloves garlic, crushed
  ½ tsp salt

Scoop the flesh from the avocados and mash it roughly with a fork. Add all the remaining ingredients, seasoning gradually with the salt to taste. Serve with corn chips, tortilla chips, or sliced vegetables.

Guacamole ▶

Stuffed Anaheim Chiles

Serves 4

Anaheim chiles are large, sweet, and ideal for stuffing. Their mild flavor complements a slightly spicy filling; these are stuffed with a lentil dal, but I sometimes used minced lamb with toasted nuts. Don't peel the chiles—the skin will be easy to peel off once cooked if you do not wish to eat it.

1 onion, chopped finely
1 Tbsp oil
1 tsp ground allspice
½ tsp chile powder
½ cup red lentils
14-oz can chopped tomatoes
¾ cup water or stock
½ tsp salt
4 Anaheim chiles
¾ cup soft goat's cheese

Cook the onion in the oil until softened but not browned, then add the spices and cook slowly for another minute. Stir in the lentils, tomatoes, and water, then season with the salt. Bring to a boil then simmer for about 30 minutes, until the lentils are soft. Season to taste, adding extra salt if necessary.

Preheat an oven to 400°F. Cut the chiles in half lengthwise and remove the membranes and seeds. Place the shells in a roasting pan, then fill them with the lentil mixture and top with spoonfuls of the goat's cheese.

Bake the chiles in the preheated oven for 30 minutes, until the cheese has melted and browned and the chiles are tender. Serve immediately.

Tortilla Wheels with Pineapple Salsa

Serves 6–8

Tortillas make excellent appetizers because they can be stuffed, sliced, and baked. These tortilla wheels may also be served plain as finger food

Filling
¾ cup cream cheese
1 green chile, seeded and chopped finely
2 Tbsps freshly chopped cilantro
4 tomatoes, seeded and chopped finely
4 scallions, chopped finely
1 bell pepper, red or yellow, seeded and chopped finely
1 cup grated Cheddar cheese
Salt and freshly ground black pepper

8 flour tortillas

Salsa
1 Tbsp black mustard seeds
1 orange
4 thick slices pineapple, fresh or canned
1 small red onion, chopped finely
1 small green chile, seeded and chopped finely
2 tomatoes, diced

Beat the cream cheese until smooth, then add all the other ingredients for the filling. Mix well and season to taste with salt and pepper. Divide the mixture between the tortillas, spreading it evenly. Place each tortilla on top of another, making 4 stacks of 2, then roll them up tightly. Cover in plastic wrap and chill for at least 2 hours.

Prepare the salsa while the tortilla rolls are chilling. Heat a nonstick skillet until evenly hot, then add the mustard seeds and cook for 1 to 2 minutes, until the seeds begin to pop. Allow to cool. Grate the rind from the orange, then peel it and chop the flesh. Mix the orange with the mustard seeds and all the other ingredients, seasoning to taste with salt and pepper. Allow the salsa to stand until required.

Preheat an oven to 400°F. Unwrap the tortillas and trim away the ends, then cut each roll into 8 slices. Place on baking sheets and bake in the preheated oven for 15–20 minutes, until well browned. Serve hot with the pineapple salsa.

▲ Tortilla Wheels with Pineapple Salsa

Cheese Peppers

This is a simple but attractive idea. A slice from each of the red and green peppers make a colorful appetizer.

1 cup mixed shelled nuts (peanuts, cashews, almonds, etc.)
Salt
Cayenne pepper
1 cup lowfat cream cheese
1 clove garlic, crushed
Freshly ground black pepper
1 medium red bell pepper
1 medium green bell pepper
Whole-wheat toast

Heat a nonstick skillet over a medium heat until evenly hot, then add the nuts and cook until browned on all sides. Scatter some salt and cayenne over some kitchen towels, add the hot nuts and toss in the seasonings. Toss occasionally until completely cooled, then chop the nuts roughly.

Beat the cream cheese until smooth, then add the garlic and nuts. Season to taste with extra salt, if necessary, and black pepper. Cut the tops from the peppers and remove the seeds and cores. Rinse the peppers to remove any loose seeds. Pack the filling into the peppers, pressing it down firmly with the back of a spoon.

Chill the peppers for 2 to 3 hours before slicing. Serve one slice of each colored pepper to each person, with lots of freshly cooked whole-wheat toast.

◄ Cheese Peppers

Brie Quesadillas

These Mexican-style snacks may be eaten either as an appetizer or as a light meal—allow 1 per person as an appetizer and 2 for a more substantial snack. They may be baked, but I find that the tortillas become a bit too crispy, so I prefer to cook them in a skillet, then under the broiler. They may be kept warm in a very low oven. They could also be served open, cut into wedges like a pizza.

Flour tortillas

For each tortilla
2–3 Tbsps refried beans
1½ oz ripe brie, cut into slivers
Chopped avocado, pickled jalapenos, and tomato salsa

Spread half of each tortilla with the refried beans, then top with the brie. Preheat a nonstick skillet and add the tortilla. Shake over the heat until the cheese begins to melt.

Meanwhile, preheat the broiler. Finish heating the tortilla through under the broiler, until the cheese has melted and the beans are hot. If possible keep the uncovered tortilla away from the heat to prevent it from becoming crispy.

Top the cheese with chopped avocado, pickled jalapeno slices, and tomato salsa, then fold the quesadilla into a "D" shape to serve.

salads and appetizers

Crab Balls with Sweet Lime Sauce

Serves 4

I use canned white crab meat to make these crab balls; it is quick and convenient. If you can get fresh white crab meat, use that. The lime sauce is only very slightly sweet, so prepare to have your taste buds roused!

Sauce
Grated rind and juice of 2 limes
1 Tbsp raw sugar
1 red chile, seeded and very finely chopped

8-oz can white crab meat, drained and
   squeezed dry
1 cup fresh whole-wheat bread crumbs
4 scallions, trimmed and very finely chopped
Salt and freshly ground black pepper
Freshly grated nutmeg
1 large egg, beaten
⅓ cup sunflower oil for frying

Mix all the ingredients for the sauce together and set aside until needed.

Mix the crab meat with the bread crumbs and scallions then season with salt, pepper, and nutmeg. Add the egg and blend the mixture together. Shape into 20 walnut-sized pieces—you may have to flour your hands to do this.

Heat the oil in a skillet and add the crab balls. Fry them for 4 to 5 minutes until evenly browned all over, turning occasionally. Drain on paper towels, then serve immediately with the lime sauce for dipping.

◀ Crab Balls with Sweet Lime Sauce

Wild Rice Stuffed Mushrooms

Serves 4

Field mushrooms make delicious appetizers when filled with a well-flavored stuffing. Serve one mushroom per person on freshly cooked, buttered whole-wheat toast. Add the mushroom stalks to a soup, or to your homemade broth.

⅓ cup wild rice
1 cup finely chopped watercress
⅔ cup lowfat cottage cheese
4 scallions, trimmed and chopped
Salt and freshly ground black pepper
4 large field mushrooms, peeled
Olive oil
Paprika
4 slices freshly cooked whole-wheat toast

Bring the rice to a boil in a pan of water, then simmer for 30–40 minutes until tender. Drain thoroughly and allow to cool slightly.

Mix the rice with the chopped watercress, cottage cheese, and scallions; season the mixture to taste. Preheat a broiler. Remove the stalks from the mushrooms and brush the shells lightly with oil. Heat for 3 to 4 minutes under the hot broiler until almost cooked. Pile the filling into the mushroom shells, then cook for a further 3 to 4 minutes, until the filling is set and hot.

Sprinkle a little paprika over the mushrooms and serve immediately on hot, lightly buttered whole-wheat toast.

main dishes

A high-fiber diet based on grains and legumes may appear to be little different from a vegetarian eating pattern but not all high fiber disciples have forsaken meat. I am a meat eater but, like so many other people, I now eat significantly less meat than I used to. By following a high-fiber diet and incorporating recipes that not only taste good but are also varied in style and texture, I do not miss the greater quantity of meat that I ate in the past.

Several of the dishes included here contain a mixture of meat or poultry and high-fiber foods. For example, in place of the classic Beef Bourgignon, which is often rich and heavy, I have included a Chicken and Lima Bean Bourgignon. The chicken contains less fat than beef and the beans mean that you need less chicken in each helping, creating a very healthy alternative to the classic beef recipe.

Some of these dishes contain pasta and it makes sense to use a whole-wheat variety in a high-fiber diet. I have yet to find an acceptable commercial whole-wheat pasta—so many of them resemble cardboard in every way—so I have made my own pasta for these recipes. Providing that you use a fin e whole-wheat flour, the pasta is easy to make, but a bread flour will be too coarse and the bran will tear the dough. As none of the recipes rely on the pasta for all their fiber, a regular white pasta will not ruin the fiber content of the dish.

I have not included any recipes for baked potatoes in this book, but they are certainly a very useful high-fiber food. If you feel your main dish is short of the essential ingredient, then serve a baked potato with it and eat the skin. However, a baked potato without butter or sour cream is like a tomato without salt, so watch the calories.

Chicken and Cannellini Bean Risotto

Serves 4

A good risotto should be moist and creamy. You should always use arborio rice. This special rice absorbs more liquid than others, which gives the correct texture to the finished dish.

½ cup cannellini or white kidney beans, soaked overnight OR
14-oz can cannellini beans
2 chicken breasts or 4 chicken thighs, skinned, boned, and diced
1 Tbsp olive oil
1 large onion, chopped
1 red bell pepper, seeded and chopped
2 plump cloves garlic, sliced finely
2 cups arborio rice, white or brown
5 cups well-flavored chicken or vegetable broth
1 cup dry white wine
1 cup frozen peas
Salt and freshly ground black pepper
2 Tbsps freshly chopped flat-leafed parsley

Drain the beans then rinse them thoroughly under cold running water. Place in a pan of fresh water, bring to a boil then cover and simmer for 1–1¼ hours, until tender.

Brown the chicken in the oil in a large skillet, then add the onion and cook until soft but not browned. Stir in the pepper and garlic, then cook for a further 2 minutes. Add the rice, toss it in the juices, then cook for 1 minute. Add 2 cups of broth and bring to a boil, stirring all the time, then simmer until the broth is absorbed, stirring occasionally. Add 2 more cups of broth and cook until absorbed, then add the wine and repeat the process for a second time.

Stir the frozen peas into the risotto with the remaining broth and cook, stirring constantly, until the broth is almost absorbed and the risotto is thick and creamy. Season to taste, then stir in the parsley just before serving.

Corn Mexicali

Serves 4

Corn on the cob can make a very filling appetizer. I like to serve it as a main course, in a tomato sauce. You will need a strong, sharp knife to cut through the corn.

4 large ears of corn, husked
4 Tbsps oil
1 onion, chopped finely
1 tsp mild chile powder
1 tsp ground cumin
1 plump clove garlic, crushed
1 green bell pepper, seeded and chopped
2 14-oz cans chopped tomatoes
Salt and freshly ground black pepper
2 Tbsps freshly chopped cilantro leaf
Tortillas or corn chips

Cut the ears of corn into slices approximately 1-inch thick. Heat 2 tablespoons of oil in a large skillet, add the corn slices, and cook quickly on both sides until they start to brown. Remove from the pan with a slotted spoon.

Heat the remaining oil in the skillet; add the onion and cook until it starts to brown, then add the spices and cook for another minute over low heat. Stir in the garlic, pepper, and tomatoes and bring the sauce to a boil.

Return the browned corn to the pan and simmer for 30 minutes, turning the slices over once during the cooking time.

Remove the corn slices to a warmed serving dish. Cook the sauce quickly until reduced and thickened, then season it to taste with salt and pepper. Add the cilantro; pour the sauce over the corns and serve immediately with tortillas, Mexican rice, refried beans, or corn chips.

Chicken and Cannellini Bean Risotto ▶

Garbanzo Beans with Sesame Sauce

This dramatically different vegetarian dish of garbanzo beans is strongly and unusually flavored, guaranteed to revitalize the most jaded of palates.

1½ cups garbanzo beans, soaked overnight
2 large onions, sliced finely
2 Tbsps fruity olive oil
2 tsps ground cumin
1 tsp ground allspice
1 red chile, seeded and sliced
4 large cloves garlic, sliced finely
6 large tomatoes, seeded and chopped, OR
14-oz can chopped tomatoes
1 cup dry white wine
1½ cups well-flavored vegetable broth
Salt and freshly ground black pepper
¼ cup sesame seeds, toasted
1 Tbsp sesame seeds, toasted
1 Tbsp tahini

Garnish
2 Tbsps freshly chopped mint
Grated rind of 1 lemon
1 large clove garlic, chopped finely

Preheat oven to 325°F. Cook the onions in the olive oil in a flameproof casserole dish until soft but not browned, then add the cumin, allspice, chile, and garlic and continue cooking over low heat for 1 or 2 minutes. Drain and rinse the garbanzo beans under cold running water, then add them with the tomatoes, white wine, and enough broth to just cover the garbanzo beans. Season well with salt and pepper, then cover the casserole and transfer it to the preheated oven for 1½ hours.

Stir the toasted sesame seeds and tahini into the casserole and season as necessary with more salt and pepper. Mix the garnish together, then sprinkle it over the casserole before serving.

◄ Garbanzo Beans with Sesame Sauce

Bean and Vegetable Pasties

Pasties are the traditional food of the mining community of Cornwall, southwest England. Originally made with shin of beef and root vegetables, the pasties had the miners' initials in pastry on them—not for garnish, but to show ownership. These bean and vegetable pasties make a good vegetarian alternative to the traditional meat pies of Cornwall.

⅓ cup mung beans, soaked overnight

Pastry
1 stick butter
1 cup fine whole-wheat flour
Pinch of salt

1 onion, chopped finely
¾ cup finely diced mixed root vegetables
½ cup finely diced Cheddar cheese
Salt and freshly ground black pepper
1 Tbsp freshly chopped mixed herbs (optional)

Drain the beans and rinse them thoroughly under cold running water. Bring to a boil in a pan of fresh water, then simmer for 30 minutes, until tender. Drain and set aside until needed.

Preheat an oven to 400°F. Prepare the pastry by blending the butter into the flour and salt. Add sufficient warm water to give a firm but workable dough, then knead lightly on a floured surface. Divide the dough into 4 and roll out into 6-inch diameter circles—use a small plate to cut around.

Mix the mung beans with all the remaining ingredients and divide the mixture between the pastry circles. Damp the edges with water, then draw the pastry together over the filling, pinching the edges together to seal them. Place the pasties on a lightly oiled baking sheet. Cook in the preheated oven for 30–35 minutes, until the pastry is crisp. Serve hot or cold.

Chicken and Vegetable Fricassee

Serves 4

Adding a variety of vegetables to a small amount of chicken makes a delicious fricassee, a lot less rich than the traditional all-chicken or chicken-and-mushroom alternative. The chicken may be replaced by cooked beans if preferred.

1 Tbsp oil
1 cup cooked chicken, shredded
4 cups prepared mixed vegetables, diced or sliced
½ cup dry white wine
1 cup sour cream
Salt and freshly ground black pepper
Freshly chopped parsley

Heat the oil in a skillet; add the chicken and cook quickly until starting to brown, then add the prepared vegetables, tossing them in the hot juices. Cover the skillet and cook slowly for about 8–10 minutes, until the vegetables have softened in the steam.

Pour the wine into the skillet and cook quickly, stirring all the time, until the wine has reduced by half. Stir in the sour cream, season to taste, then heat gently without boiling. Serve on a bed of rice, garnished with chopped parsley.

Chestnut and Cranberry Casserole

Serves 6–8

This is a dish of surprising flavors—slightly sweet and sour and full of bright colors and textures. The casserole requires very little cooking, as the vegetables should still be slightly crunchy and retain their color. If serving on a bed of brown rice, the whole dish can be cooked in the time that it takes to boil the rice.

1 leek, sliced
1 Tbsp oil
1 pound peeled chestnuts, fresh or frozen
1 red bell pepper, seeded and chopped
1 zucchini, quartered and sliced thickly
4 sticks celery, chopped roughly
⅓ cup raisins
1 Tbsp soy sauce
1 Tbsp freshly chopped cilantro
1 cinnamon stick, broken
2 cups well-flavored vegetable broth
3 cups (8 oz) fresh cranberries
2 Tbsps raw sugar
Soy sauce to taste
Freshly chopped cilantro to garnish

Cook the leek in the oil until softened but not browned, then add the chestnuts and stir over the heat until defrosted, if frozen. Add the pepper, zucchini, and celery; stir-fry for 1 minute, then stir in all the remaining ingredients except the cranberries and sugar.

Bring the casserole to a boil, then simmer gently for 10–15 minutes. Add the cranberries; continue to cook for a further 10 minutes. Remove the cinnamon stick and add about 2 tablespoons of sugar. Stir in extra soy sauce to taste. Serve on a bed of boiled rice, topped with chopped cilantro.

Chestnut and Cranberry Casserole ▶

Lentil and Pumpkin Lasagne

Serves 6

Pumpkin and lentils make a satisfying alternative to the traditional meat filling for lasagne. Use homemade or pre-cooked lasagne for this dish.

 1 large onion, chopped finely
 2 Tbsps olive oil
 1 zucchini, diced
 1 green bell pepper, seeded and diced
 1–2 cloves garlic, crushed
 1 pound pumpkin purée, fresh or canned
 3/4 cup red lentils
 14-oz can chopped tomatoes
 3 cups well-flavored vegetable broth
 Salt and freshly ground black pepper
 2 Tbsp freshly chopped mixed herbs
 Fresh whole-wheat lasagne made with 1 cup fine
   whole-wheat flour and 1 large egg
 OR 6 large sheets whole-wheat lasagne
 1½ cups ricotta cheese
 1½ cups sour cream
 1 cup grated Cheddar cheese, loosely packed

Cook the onion in the oil until softened but not browned, then stir in the zucchini and pepper and cook for another 2 minutes. Add the garlic, pumpkin purée, lentils, and tomatoes and stir well. Add the broth, herbs, and seasonings, then bring the sauce to a boil. Simmer for 20–25 minutes, until the lentils are soft and the sauce has thickened.

Preheat an oven to 400°F. Prepare the pasta by mixing together the flour and egg, then process it through a pasta machine into 6 thin strips of lasagne. Bring a large pan of water to a boil and cook the lasagne quickly, 2 or 3 sheets at a time, for 1 to 2 minutes, until it floats to the top of the pan. Drain.

Place half the lentil mixture in the bottom of a suitable buttered ovenproof dish and top with half the pasta. Repeat the layers. Mix the ricotta and sour cream together and season with salt and pepper. Add half the cheese, then spread the mixture over the lasagne, topping it with the remaining cheese.

Bake the lasagne in the preheated oven for 30–40 minutes, until the topping is set and brown.

Lentils and Rice

Serves 4–6

This is a filling dish which may be served by itself or with a green salad. Often known as kedgeree, it is usually made with smoked haddock. This variation is a good way of using up leftover green or brown lentils, but is just as good when made with canned lentils.

 1½ cups brown rice
 1 large onion, sliced finely
 1–2 Tbsp curry powder, according to taste
 3 Tbsps olive oil
 1 cup cooked or canned lentils, drained
 Salt and freshly ground black pepper
 2 hard-boiled eggs, chopped
 3 Tbsps heavy cream
 1–2 Tbsps freshly chopped cilantro

Place the rice in a large pan of water; bring to a boil and simmer for 30 minutes, or until the rice is just tender. Drain.

Cook the onion with the curry powder in the oil over low heat until the onion is soft, then stir in the cooked rice and lentils. Cook for 2 to 3 minutes until piping hot, then add the chopped eggs and the cream, if used. Cook for a further 1 to 2 minutes.

Season well, then stir in the cilantro leaves and serve immediately.

Lentil and Pumpkin Lasagne ▶

Vegetable Tortillas with Mixed Bean Salsa

Serves 4

Flour tortillas are quite easy to make at home but they do take time, so I often use ready-made tortillas, which just need heating through for a minute or two. Don't overfill the tortillas—they are meant to be eaten in your fingers, but a generous filling may necessitate a knife and fork!

Salsa

15-oz can mixed beans, drained and rinsed
1 red onion, chopped finely
2 cloves garlic, chopped finely
1 cup diced cucumber
1 red chile, seeded and finely chopped
1 avocado, chopped
1 Tbsp orange juice
1 Tbsp white wine vinegar
Salt and freshly ground black pepper

2 Tbsps olive oil
6 cups diced mixed vegetables (leeks, onions, celery, mushrooms, bell peppers, etc.)
1 tsp chile powder
14 oz can chopped tomatoes
Salt and freshly ground black pepper

Serve with:

8 flour tortillas, warmed
Grated Cheddar cheese
Sour cream

Prepare the salsa by mixing all the ingredients together and then leaving for up to an hour, to allow the flavors to blend.

Heat the oil in a large skillet or wok; add all the prepared vegetables and stir-fry quickly for 2 to 3 minutes. Stir in the chile powder and the tomatoes and cook for a further 5 minutes, until the vegetables are just softened. Season to taste.

To serve the tortillas, allow each person to spread some of the vegetable mixture over a tortilla, then top it with grated cheese. Add a spoonful of salsa and a dollop of sour cream. Roll up and eat carefully with your fingers. Knives and forks are advisable for anyone that is wearing their best outfit!

Hazelnut and Zucchini Pasta

Serves 4

Whole-wheat pasta is easy to make if you use fine whole-wheat flour—the bran in bread flour is too coarse for good pasta and the dough will not hold together. Use prepared pasta if you prefer, allowing about 4 ounces per person.

2 Tbsps butter
2–3 Tbsps olive oil
4–6 zucchini, sliced diagonally (try to use a mixture of green and golden)
2–3 plump cloves garlic, crushed
¾ cup hazelnuts, toasted and chopped roughly
¾ cup freshly grated Parmesan cheese
Salt and freshly ground black pepper

Pasta

2 cups fine whole-wheat flour
2 medium eggs
OR prepared whole-wheat tagliatelle

Heat the butter and oil together; add the zucchini slices and cook over a medium high heat until browned and softened. This takes about 12–15 minutes. Add the garlic and hazelnuts to the pan once the zucchini have started to soften.

Mix the flour with the eggs to make a firm pasta dough. Knead thoroughly, then process through a pasta machine and cut into tagliatelle. Bring a large pan of salted water to a boil; add the pasta and boil quickly for 2 to 3 minutes, until just tender. If using prepared pasta, cook as instructed on the back of the packet.

Drain the pasta, shake briefly, then add to the zucchini mixture in the pan. Toss well, seasoning with salt and pepper, then toss in the Parmesan, which will melt over the hot pasta. Serve immediately, while still hot.

Hazelnut and Zucchini Pasta ▶

Chicken and Sweet Potato Curry

Serves 4

I love cooking curries at home. They do not take very long to prepare because they are mainly stir fried. The ingredients for the sauce should be blended to a thick paste before cooking. The sweet potato in this recipe makes the chicken go further, and the curry should be served with boiled rice or chapatis (see page 193). This curry is mild—add an extra chile or a little more curry powder if you wish.

Sauce
1 large onion
3 cloves garlic
1 green chile, seeded and chopped roughly
2 Tbsps tomato paste
1 Tbsp mild curry powder
1 Tbsp lime pickle or spiced fruit chutney
1 tsp raw sugar
1 tsp salt
1-inch piece fresh ginger root, peeled and chopped

2 chicken breast fillets, skinned and diced
3 Tbsps sunflower oil
2 cups diced sweet potato
2 cups water
⅓ cup fresh cilantro leaves, torn

Purée all the ingredients for the sauce together in a blender or food processor until a thick paste forms. Cook the chicken in the oil in a large skillet until it starts to brown, then add the sweet potato and cook until lightly browned all over.

Spoon the curry paste into the skillet and cook slowly for 2 to 3 minutes. Stir in the water. Simmer slowly for 20–25 minutes, until the chicken is tender. Add a little more water, if necessary, during cooking. Season to taste with salt, then add the cilantro and serve.

◀ Chicken and Sweet Potato Curry

Pasta Prima Verde

Serves 4

This is a celebration of the first months of summer when asparagus, peas, and beans are small, bright green and full of flavor. Perfect summer food.

1 cup sugar snaps or snow peas, topped and tailed
1 cup fine green beans, topped, tailed and halved
1½ cups asparagus, trimmed and cut into 2 inch lengths
1 cup shelled fava beans
1 small leek, sliced finely
1 Tbsp butter
1 cup heavy cream

Pasta
2 cups fine whole-wheat flour
2 large eggs, beaten
OR prepared whole-wheat pasta

1–2 Tbsps freshly chopped parsley

Bring a large pan of salted water to a boil. Cook the sugar snaps, beans, and asparagus individually, plunging them into iced water immediately to prevent over-cooking. Cook the sugar snaps for 2 minutes; fine green beans for 1 minute; asparagus stalks for 3 minutes, then add the tips and cook for a further 2 minutes; and the fava beans for 3 minutes.

Cook the leek slowly in the butter until soft but not brown, then add the cream and heat until almost boiling. Drain the vegetables and add them to the pan then heat gently for 2–3 minutes until piping hot. Stir in the parsley.

Cook the pasta in a large pan of boiling salted water, then drain and shake dry. Add the pasta to the vegetables, tossing it in the cream, and serve immediately.

main dishes

Adzuki and Fennel Casserole

Serves 6

Adzuki beans are very popular in Chinese cookery. This casserole combines some of the most popular flavorings of Chinese cuisine with the more gutsy flavorings of the Pacific Rim. The orange salsa makes a perfect accompaniment.

Salsa

1 orange
2 tomatoes, chopped
½ red onion or 4 scallions, chopped finely
1 small green chile, seeded and chopped finely
1 clove garlic, chopped finely
1 Tbsp freshly chopped cilantro
1 green bell pepper, seeded and chopped
Salt and freshly ground black pepper

1 cup adzuki beans, soaked overnight and drained
1 onion, chopped finely
1 bulb fennel, sliced finely
1 Tbsp oil
1 red chile, seeded and chopped finely
1-inch piece ginger root, peeled and sliced finely
2 cloves garlic, sliced finely
1 tsp 5-Spice powder
1 cinnamon stick, broken
½ tsp cloves
1 piece lemon grass, chopped very finely
1 cup orange juice
14-oz can chopped tomatoes
8-oz can water chestnuts, drained and sliced
Soy sauce to taste

Prepare the salsa by grating the rind from the orange and then chopping the flesh. Mix with the remaining ingredients and half the bell pepper.

Drain the beans and rinse under cold water. Cook the onion and fennel in the oil until soft but not browned, then add the chile, ginger root, garlic, spices, and lemon grass. Cook slowly for 1 to 2 minutes, stirring, then add the beans, orange juice, and tomatoes. Bring to a boil, cover, and simmer gently for 30 minutes. Stir in the remaining chopped pepper and the water chestnuts and continue cooking for a further 10–15 minutes, until the beans are tender. Season to taste with soy sauce and serve with the salsa.

Chicken and Lima Bean Bourgignon

Serves 4

Beef Bourgignon, the traditional dish of Burgundy, is rich and heavy—delicious, but often not to the taste of the health-conscious diner. This recipe uses a mixture of chicken and beans for a lighter dish.

⅔ cup lima beans, soaked overnight
1 Tbsp olive oil
1 Tbsp butter
4 chicken thighs
1 large onion, chopped finely
2 strips bacon, diced
½ cup brandy
2 cloves garlic, crushed
4 sprigs fresh thyme
2 bay leaves
1 bouquet garni
Salt and freshly ground black pepper
1 Tbsp tomato paste
2 cups full-bodied red wine
1 cup sliced button mushrooms
Sour cream and freshly chopped chives to garnish

Preheat oven to 350°F. Rinse the beans thoroughly then bring to a boil in a pan of fresh water. Simmer until required.

Heat the oil and butter together in a flameproof casserole, then add the chicken thighs and cook quickly until browned all over. Remove the chicken with a slotted spoon; add the onion and bacon and cook until softened but not browned. Return the chicken to the casserole and remove the pan from heat. Warm the brandy gently until it ignites. Pour the brandy into the pan and leave until the flames subside, then return the pan to the heat and add the garlic, herbs, and seasonings. Mix the tomato paste with the wine and pour into the pan, adding a little stock, if necessary, to cover the chicken. Bring to a boil, then cover the pan and cook in the preheated oven for 1½ hours.

Stir the mushrooms into the casserole; check the seasoning and that the beans are tender. Return the casserole to the oven for a further 15–20 minutes. Garnish with sour cream and chives.

◀ Chicken and Lima Bean Bourgignon

Ham and Cheese Vegetable Cobbler

Serves 6

An excellent way of using up the leftovers from a large ham at Christmas or Thanksgiving. Turkey, chicken, or lamb would work just as well as ham, and you could really use any vegetables that you have on hand—I don't cook them before adding them to the sauce, so they remain a little more crunchy after cooking.

1 onion, chopped finely
1 leek, trimmed and sliced finely
3 stalks celery, sliced
1½ cups ham, chopped
⅔ cup whole almonds (salted)

Sauce
2 Tbsps butter or margarine
2 Tbsps fine whole-wheat flour
2 cups milk
Salt and freshly ground black pepper
1 Tbsp whole grain mustard

Topping
½ cup whole-wheat flour
½ tsp salt
½ stick butter
1 cup All-Bran cereal
⅔ cup grated Cheddar cheese

Preheat oven to 375°F. Mix the prepared vegetables with the ham and almonds and place in an ovenproof dish. Melt the margarine or butter in a pan, then stir in the flour and cook slowly for 1 to 2 minutes. Gradually add the milk off the heat, then bring the sauce slowly to a boil and simmer for 1 to 2 minutes. Season the sauce to taste and add the mustard; pour it over the prepared vegetables and ham and mix carefully.

Mix the flour and salt together for the topping, then blend in the butter. Stir in the All-Bran and cheese. Spoon the topping over the ham mixture, smoothing the top.

Bake the cobbler in the preheated oven for 45 minutes, until the topping has browned. Serve hot with a green salad.

Millet and Vegetable Gratin

Serves 6

Tell your friends that you are serving millet and they will be amazed. Once they have eaten it, however, they will be delighted.

2 cups millet, washed
1 large carrot, sliced finely
1 onion, sliced finely
8 strips bacon, chopped finely
2 cups sliced button mushrooms
2 cups thick tomato juice
Salt and freshly ground black pepper
2 Tbsps fresh basil leaves, roughly torn
½ cup grated Cheddar cheese

Preheat oven to 375°F. Add the millet to a large pan of boiling water and simmer for 20 minutes, then drain. Cook the carrot and the onion with the bacon until they start to soften, then add the sliced mushrooms. Cook for a further five minutes until all the vegetables are soft.

Add the tomato juice and the drained millet, then season well with salt and pepper and add the basil. Pack into a buttered, ovenproof dish, then bake in the preheated oven for 40 minutes. Scatter the cheese over the millet, then return the dish to the oven for a further 30 minutes. Serve hot with a spicy tomato sauce or chutney.

Curried Vegetable Casserole ▶

Curried Vegetable Casserole

Serves 6

This is a famous dish of the Cape region of South Africa, where it is called *Bobotie*. Traditionally made with ground beef, this variation has all the spiciness of the meat dish.

2 onions, sliced finely
2 Tbsps sunflower oil
1 Tbsp medium curry powder
1 tsp ground turmeric
6 cups mixed diced root vegetables (e.g., turnips, yellow turnips, parsnips, carrots)
2 Tbsps white wine vinegar
1 Tbsp dark brown sugar
1 tsp salt
½ tsp freshly ground black pepper
1 thick slice whole-wheat bread
⅔ cup seedless raisins
3 Tbsps fruit chutney
½ cup water
4–5 lime leaves (optional)
⅓ cup shredded almonds
1 large egg, beaten
⅔ cup milk

Preheat an oven to 350°F.

Cook the onion in the oil until it begins to soften, then stir in the curry powder and the turmeric and cook for a further 1 to 2 minutes over a low heat. Add the prepared root vegetables, vinegar, sugar, salt, and pepper and cook gently over low heat until the vegetables begin to soften.

Soak the bread in water for 3 to 4 minutes, then drain it, squeeze it dry, and add it to the vegetables. Stir in the raisins, chutney, and water, then pack the mixture into a buttered ovenproof dish. Bury the lime leaves in the mixture and cover the dish with buttered foil. Bake in the preheated oven for 1½ hours. Reduce the oven temperature to 300°F.

Remove the foil from the dish and sprinkle the almonds over the vegetables. Beat the egg with the milk, adding extra milk if necessary to make 1 cup. Pour it over the vegetables; bake for a further 30 minutes at the lower temperature, until the custard has set. Serve with mango chutney and a mixed salad.

Spinach and Walnut Whole-Wheat Quiche

Serves 4–6

The fillings in vegetable quiches can easily become one dull mass of indistinguishable textures. In this quiche, I have mixed walnuts with the spinach, giving a good crunch to the filling.

Pastry
1 stick butter
1¼ cups fine whole-wheat flour
Pinch of salt

Filling
1 pound frozen chopped leaf spinach
Salt and freshly ground black pepper
Freshly grated nutmeg
⅔ cup walnut pieces, roughly chopped
½ cup blue cheese, crumbled (Stilton or Danish)
1¼ cups milk
2 large eggs

Preheat oven to 400°F. Blend the butter with the flour and salt in a bowl until the mixture resembles fine bread crumbs. Mix to a manageable dough with warm water, then roll out and use the pastry to line a 9-inch loose-bottomed pie pan. Line with paper towels then fill with baking beans. Bake in the preheated oven for 20 minutes.

Cook the spinach gently in a covered pan until piping hot; shake from time to time to prevent it from burning. Squeeze the spinach dry then season to taste with salt, pepper, and nutmeg.

Remove the paper and beans from the pastry case and fill with a layer of the spinach, then a layer of walnuts. Crumble the blue cheese over the top of the filling.

Beat the milk and eggs and season with salt and pepper. Pour the custard over the spinach filling then grate a little nutmeg over the top. Reduce the oven temperature to 375°F and bake the quiche for 25–30 minutes, until the custard has set. Serve warm or cold.

Rich Ratatouille and Goat's Cheese Quiche

Serves 4-6

Fillings for quiches are almost infinitely variable and this is one of my favorites, invented to use up some leftover ratatouille. I usually use a can of vegetables for ease, and sometimes I add chopped nuts to the vegetables—about ⅓ cup—to give a little extra texture.

Pastry
¾ stick butter
¾ cup fine whole-wheat flour
Pinch of salt

14-oz can ratatouille
1 Tbsp basil leaves, roughly torn
⅔ cup soft goat's cheese
Salt and freshly ground black pepper
1¼ cups milk or milk and light cream, mixed
Salt and freshly ground black pepper
2 large eggs, beaten

Preheat oven to 400°F. Prepare the pastry by blending the butter into the flour and salt until the mixture resembles fine bread crumbs. Mix to a firm, manageable dough with warm water, then knead lightly on a floured surface and roll out to line a deep 7-inch pie pan. Chill the pastry lightly for 10–15 minutes, then line the pastry case with paper towels and fill with baking beans. Bake for 15 minutes in the preheated oven.

Remove the paper and the beans and spread the ratatouille over the partly-cooked pastry. Sprinkle the basil leaves and goat's cheese over and season with pepper. Beat together the milk, the eggs, and some seasoning, then pour the mixture into the pastry case over the vegetables and cheese. Return the quiche to the oven, reduce the heat to 375°F and cook for a further 35 minutes or until set. This quiche is best served warm.

Rich Ratatouille and Goat's Cheese Quiche ▶

Spiced
Baked Beans

This is my version of Boston baked beans. I like to add spicy sausage toward the end of cooking, but this is not essential. Do not make the dish too sweet— my husband added molasses once and it was ghastly!

1½ cups black-eyed peas, soaked overnight
1 large onion, chopped finely
2 Tbsps oil
½ tsp chile powder
½ tsp ground cumin
1–2 plump cloves garlic, sliced
1 green chile, seeded and chopped finely
14-oz can chopped tomatoes
1 cup well-flavored broth
Salt and freshly ground black pepper
1 thick pepperoni or other garlic sausage, thickly sliced
1 Tbsp wine vinegar
½–1 Tbsp raw sugar
Freshly chopped parsley to garnish

Drain the peas and rinse them thoroughly under cold running water; set aside until needed. Cook the onion in the oil until soft, then add the spices and cook slowly for another minute. Stir in the garlic, chile, and peas, then add the tomatoes and broth. Season lightly, bring to a boil, then cover and simmer for 45 minutes.

Season to taste with extra salt and pepper, then add the sliced sausage to the beans. Cover and simmer for a further 15 minutes. Season with the vinegar and sugar before garnishing with parsley.

Navy Beans
with Broccoli

Serves 4

This is a simple but tasty casserole. The secret of any bean dish is to use a good, well-flavored broth.

1½ cups navy beans, soaked overnight
1 Tbsp oil
1 onion, sliced finely
1 leek, trimmed and sliced finely
2 cups sliced button mushrooms
2 blades mace
½ cup freshly chopped parsley
1 cup dry white wine
1 cup well-flavored vegetable broth
Salt and freshly ground black pepper
½ red bell pepper, chopped finely
1 cup small broccoli florets
2 Tbsps sour cream

Preheat oven to 350°F. Drain the beans and rinse them well under cold running water.

Heat the oil in a flameproof casserole; add the onion and leek and cook until soft, then stir in the mushrooms and cook for a further 2 to 3 minutes until they soften. Add the beans, mace, half the parsley, the white wine, and sufficient vegetable broth to just cover the beans. Season lightly with salt and pepper, then bring to a boil. Cover the casserole and cook in the preheated oven for 1½ hours, until the beans are tender.

Stir the beans; most of the liquid will have been absorbed but there should still be a little at the bottom of the pan. Add extra salt and pepper then stir in the red bell pepper and broccoli. Cover the pan and return it to the oven for a further 15–20 minutes until the broccoli is just tender. Stir in the sour cream and serve with steamed carrots or a tomato salad.

main dishes

◀ Spiced Baked Beans

Millet Rissoles with Yogurt Sauce

Serves 4

Rissoles are traditionally made with leftover, cooked meats, but I have used millet to make these delicious variations on an old favorite.

¾ cup raw millet
⅔ cup milk or milk and broth, mixed
1 Tbsp butter
1 heaping Tbsp fine whole-wheat flour
Salt and freshly ground black pepper
4 scallions, chopped finely
1–2 Tbsps freshly chopped dill
1½ cups fresh whole-wheat bread crumbs

Sauce
1 tsp cumin seeds
Grated rind and juice of 1 lemon
2 Tbsps freshly chopped cilantro
1½ cups thick plain yogurt
Salt and freshly ground black pepper

For frying
2 eggs, beaten
1 cup dry or toasted bread crumbs
⅓ cup oil

Add the millet to a large pan of boiling water and simmer for 20 minutes, until soft. Meanwhile, place the milk, butter, and flour in a pan and bring to a boil, stirring constantly. Simmer the sauce for 1 to 2 minutes until thickened, then season to taste and pour into a large bowl. Drain the millet and add it to the sauce with the scallions, dill, and bread crumbs. Mix together, and allow to cool.

Shape the mixture into 12 rounds or rissoles; coat your hands in flour and toss the rissoles in the beaten eggs, then coat in the dry crumbs. Repeat this process if necessary to get a good coating.

Prepare the sauce. Toast the cumin seeds in a heavy-based skillet for 1 to 2 minutes, then crush lightly in a mortar and pestle or with the end of a rolling pin. Mix the cumin with the other sauce ingredients and place in a small pan over a very low heat to warm gently.

Heat the oil in the same skillet until hot, then add the rissoles and cook for 10–12 minutes until well-browned. Serve with the yogurt sauce.

Glamorgan Sausages

Serves 4

These vegetarian sausages originated in south Wales, where they were made with the local cheese—hence the name. The cheese has long since disappeared, but the sausages live on. Slice the leeks very finely or it will be difficult to shape the mixture correctly. Mashed potato binds the mixture well and no egg is needed.

1 cup finely sliced leeks
1 Tbsp oil
1 cup cold mashed potato
1 cup grated Cheddar or Caerphilly cheese
Salt and freshly ground black pepper
1 tsp Dijon mustard
1 Tbsp freshly chopped parsley
1 cup fresh whole-wheat bread crumbs

2–3 Tbsps olive oil for frying
Chutney or relish to serve

Cook the leek in the oil until soft but not browned, then mix with all the remaining ingredients, adding sufficient bread crumbs to make a very stiff dough. Divide into 8 then shape into sausages, flouring your hands to make it easy to handle the mixture.

Heat the oil for frying in a skillet; add the sausages and cook quickly for 6 to 8 minutes, turning carefully to brown on all sides. Serve with a spicy fruit chutney or relish.

Glamorgan Sausages ▶

Cracked Wheat Pilaf

Serves 4

I often use a very coarse cracked wheat in this dish as it gives a good, nutty texture. The wheat makes a welcome change from rice.

1 large onion, sliced
1 leek, trimmed and sliced
2 Tbsps olive oil
1 tsp ground cumin
1 tsp ground ginger
1–2 plump cloves garlic, sliced finely
4 stalks celery, trimmed and sliced
1 red bell pepper, seeded and sliced
1 cup baby corn, halved
1½ cups cracked wheat
14-oz can chopped tomatoes
3 cups water or broth
Salt and freshly ground black pepper
1 cup snow peas, topped and tailed
6 halves sun-dried tomatoes, shredded

Cook the onion and leek in the oil until softened but not browned, then add the spices and cook for another minute. Add the garlic, celery, pepper, and corn, then cook briefly before stirring the cracked wheat into the pan. Add the tomatoes, broth, and seasonings, then simmer for 12–15 minutes, stirring occasionally. Add the snow peas and sun-dried tomatoes and cook for a further 4 to 5 minutes. Serve with a tossed green salad.

Spinach and Pancetta Risotto

Serves 4

I love risotto—it is so versatile and a very special dish can be made with very simple ingredients. I first made this when I had masses of spinach in the garden and the color of the risotto is fantastic. Omit the pancetta if you wish, but I like to pile it on top of the rice with some shavings of Parmesan before serving.

¾ cup finely finely sliced onion (1 large)
3 Tbsps olive oil
2 cloves garlic, crushed
1½ cups risotto or arborio rice
5 cups well-flavored vegetable broth
Salt and freshly ground black pepper
Freshly grated nutmeg
6 cups leaf spinach, shredded coarsely
5 slices pancetta
Parmesan cheese shavings to serve

Cook the onion in the oil until softened but not brown, then add the garlic and rice and cook over a low heat for a further 1 minute. Add one third of the stock then stir gently until it has been absorbed, then add half the remainder and simmer again.

Season the risotto well then add the spinach with the remaining stock and cook until the spinach has wilted and the stock has almost been absorbed. Stir-fry the pancetta in a dry non-stick skillet until crispy, then serve it on top of the risotto, garnished with slivers of Parmesan.

◀ Cracked Wheat Pilaf

Sweet and Sour Vegetable Stir-Fry

Serves 4

Stir-frying is a very quick method of cooking—what takes the time is preparing all the vegetables before you start! It is important to have everything chopped before you begin cooking or the finished dish will be rather overcooked. Put the rice on to boil before chopping the other ingredients, then stir-fry and rice should both be ready at the same time. All the prepared vegetables should be approximately the same size for even cooking.

1½ cups brown rice

1 cup carrot matchsticks
1 red onion, chopped
1 cup baby corn, halved
4 sticks celery, chopped
1 leek, sliced
2 cups shredded bok choy
2 Tbsps sunflower or peanut oil

Sauce
⅔ cup pineapple juice
1 Tbsp raw sugar
¼ cup white wine vinegar
¼ cup tomato ketchup
Pinch of salt
Cilantro leaves and Soy sauce

Bring the rice to a boil in a large pan of water, then simmer for 30 minutes or until tender.

Meanwhile, prepare all the vegetables. Heat the oil in a large skillet or wok, then add the carrots, onion, corns, celery, and leek and stir-fry for 4 to 5 minutes, until starting to soften but still crisp. Blend the ingredients for the sauce together and add to the pan with the bok choy. Continue stir-frying for 2 to 3 minutes until the cabbage begins to wilt. Stir in the cilantro at the last moment.

Serve the stir-fry on a bed of the freshly cooked rice and spoon the sauce over. Provide soy sauce separately for people to add if desired.

Quick Bean Pot

Serves 6

Bean dishes made with dried beans require some careful forward planning, but this one can be made quickly in under an hour using fresh vegetables and canned beans.

1 large onion, sliced finely
2 Tbsps olive oil
1 cup sliced carrots
1 cup yellow turnip, finely diced
2 cups sliced zucchini
2 15-oz cans beans with their juice, e.g., mixed beans and red kidney beans
2 Tbsps freshly chopped oregano
Salt and freshly ground black pepper
2 Tbsps tomato paste
⅔ cup grated Cheddar cheese

Cook the onion in the oil in a large flameproof casserole dish until softened but not browned, then add the carrot and turnip and cook for 3 to 4 minutes. Stir in the zucchini, beans and juice, the seasonings, the herbs, and the tomato paste. Bring to a boil, then simmer for 30–40 minutes, until the vegetables are tender and the broth is reduced to below the level of the beans.

Preheat a broiler. Season the casserole to taste then sprinkle with the cheese. Cook under the broiler until the cheese has melted and browned.

Quick Bean Pot ▶

Shrimp Chow Mein

Serves 4

This is simple and delicious. I prefer to use fresh shrimp and to add them with the bean sprouts; but frozen shrimp may be used, although they should be added as soon as the onion has softened. The drawback with frozen shrimp is that they reduce the pan temperature dramatically and it takes a while to recover.

3 sheets (8 oz) thread egg noodles
1 large onion, chopped
2 Tbsp sunflower or peanut oil
1 tsp Chinese 5-Spice powder
1 cup zucchini matchsticks
1 cup carrot matchsticks
1 green bell pepper, seeded and cut into fine strips
1 red chile, seeded and chopped finely (optional)
2 plump cloves garlic, sliced finely
2 cups peeled shrimp
2 large handfuls bean sprouts
¼ cup sherry
¼ cup soy sauce
½ cup water

Soak the noodles in boiling water until needed, stirring them occasionally to separate the strands. Cook the onion in the oil in a large skillet until softened but not browned. Stir in the 5-Spice powder and cook for a further 1 minute.

Add the zucchini, carrots, pepper, chile, and garlic, then stir-fry for 3 to 4 minutes. Drain the noodles, then add them to the skillet with the shrimp and bean sprouts. Mix the sherry, soy sauce, and water together, then pour the mixture into the pan. Cook for 2 to 3 minutes, tossing the vegetables and noodles together in the sauce. Serve piping hot, with extra soy sauce.

▲ Shrimp Chow Mein

French Cassoulet

Serves 8

This is a classic French dish, each region claiming that it has the correct recipe. It takes a long time to make a good Cassoulet and it cannot be hurried, but it is worth the time and effort.

    2 cups navy beans, soaked overnight
    2 large onions, sliced finely
    3 Tbsps olive oil
    2 cloves garlic, crushed
    5 cups diced cooked meats, e.g., chicken, ham,
        garlic sausage, goose, duck
    Salt and freshly ground black pepper
    ½ cup freshly chopped parsley
    3 tomatoes, chopped
    4 cups well-flavored chicken or vegetable broth
    2 cups whole-wheat bread crumbs

Drain the beans and rinse them thoroughly under cold running water. Bring to a boil in a pan of fresh water, then cover and simmer for 1½ hours, until tender. Drain and keep until required.

Preheat oven to 325°F. Cook the onions in the oil in a large flameproof casserole dish until lightly browned, then add the garlic. Remove from the heat and add the meats in a thick layer, seasoning with a little salt and pepper and about half the parsley. Layer the tomatoes on top of the meats then cover with the cooked beans. Scatter the remaining parsley over with plenty of seasoning, then add the broth, which should come just below the level of the beans. Bring to a boil, then cover and bake for 1½ hours.

Remove the lid. Make a thick layer of bread crumbs over the Cassoulet then return it to the oven for a further 20–30 minutes, uncovered, until the bread crumbs have browned lightly. Serve immediately while still hot.

Chicken and Kidney Bean Gumbo

Serves 6

Gumbo is like so many traditional dishes—there are numerous recipes for it and each one claims to be The One! This is my variation on the theme, using beans to make the meat go further. Omit the shrimp if you wish.

    1 large onion, sliced finely
    3 stalks celery, trimmed and sliced
    2 Tbsps olive oil
    1 pound okra, trimmed and sliced
    2 plump cloves garlic, sliced finely
    14-oz can chopped tomatoes
    2 Tbsps butter
    3 Tbsps fine whole-wheat flour
    ½ tsp chile powder
    1 tsp ground cumin
    4 sprigs fresh thyme
    4 cups well-flavored chicken or vegetable broth
    Salt and freshly ground black pepper
    1 cup brown rice
    1 cup cooked chicken
    14-oz can kidney beans, drained
    1 cup shrimp
    Hot pepper sauce

Cook the onion and celery in the oil for about 5 minutes until starting to soften but not browned. Add the okra and garlic and cook for a further 3 minutes before adding the tomatoes. Cover the pan and simmer slowly for 15 minutes.

Prepare the sauce while the okra mixture is cooking. Melt the butter in a large flameproof casserole dish, then stir in the flour, spices, herbs, and seasonings off the heat. Cook slowly for 2 to 3 minutes then gradually add the broth, again off the heat. Bring to a boil, stirring, then simmer for 2 minutes before adding the okra mixture. Season, return to a boil, then cover and simmer for 1 hour.

After 30 minutes, bring the rice to a boil in a pan of water, then simmer for 30–40 minutes, until tender. Add the chopped chicken and kidney beans to the gumbo. Return to a boil and simmer for 10 minutes, then add the shrimp and cook for a further 5 minutes. Season to taste, adding pepper sauce as required, then serve garnished with spoonfuls of the cooked rice.

Chicken and Kidney Bean Gumbo

Caramelized Onion Tart

Serves 6–8

I call this a tart although it looks more like a pizza. It is very savory and makes a good supper dish.

- 5 cups sliced onions
- 3 Tbsps olive oil
- 6 small cloves garlic, peeled and left whole
- 3 bay leaves
- Salt and freshly ground black pepper
- 4–5 sprigs fresh thyme

Base
- ⅓ cup toasted chopped hazelnuts or almonds
- 1 cup fine whole-wheat flour
- ½ tsp salt
- 1 egg, beaten
- ¼ cup olive oil

Cook the onions in the olive oil until they start to brown, then add the garlic, herbs, and seasonings. Cook slowly for at least 1 hour, until softened and lightly browned.

Make the base by blending the dry ingredients together, then binding them with the egg and olive oil. Work into a dough, then roll out to a rough circle about 10 inches in diameter on a baking sheet. Chill for at least 45 minutes.

Preheat oven to 425°F. Remove the bay leaves from the onion mixture; spread it over the nut base. Grind some black pepper over the onions, drizzle a little extra olive oil on top and bake for 25 minutes, until the base is lightly browned. Cool slightly before serving.

Spiced Chicken with Cabbage

Serves 4

This recipe is based on an African dish of cabbage with peanut butter. It is very satisfying and should be served with plain boiled rice.

- 1 onion, sliced finely
- 1 Tbsp peanut oil
- 1½ cups cooked shredded chicken
- ½ tsp curry powder
- 1 green chile, seeded and chopped finely
- 2 cloves garlic, sliced finely
- 2 cups green beans, cut into 1-inch lengths
- 2 cups shredded white cabbage
- 1–2 Tbsp peanut butter, according to taste
- 14-oz can chopped tomatoes
- Salt and freshly ground black pepper

Cook the onion in the oil until it starts to brown, then add the chicken. Cook quickly for 2 or 3 minutes to heat the chicken through. Stir in the curry powder and cook slowly for 1 minute. Add the chile, garlic, and green beans and stir-fry for 1 to 2 minutes. Add the shredded cabbage, peanut butter, and tomatoes, then simmer for 6 to 8 minutes, until the cabbage just starts to soften. Season to taste with salt and freshly ground black pepper, then serve on a bed of boiled rice.

main dishes

◀ Caramelized Onion Tart

Brazil Nut Loaf

Serves 6

This is a soft, spicy loaf with plenty of texture. The salsa complements the flavor nicely

1 large onion
8 oz mushrooms
2 plump cloves garlic
1 Tbsp ground coriander
1 tsp ground ginger
2 Tbsps oil
7-oz can chopped tomatoes
1 Tbsp tomato paste
1½ cups brazil nuts, chopped roughly
1 cup fresh whole-wheat bread crumbs
Salt and freshly ground black pepper
1 large egg, beaten

Salsa
1 Tbsp cumin seeds
½ cucumber, diced
2 tomatoes, diced
1 mild red chile, seeded and diced
4 scallions, trimmed and sliced finely
2 plump cloves garlic, chopped finely
Salt and freshly ground black pepper
2 Tbsps white wine vinegar

Preheat an oven to 375°F and lightly grease a large loaf pan. Chop the onion in a food processor; add the mushrooms and garlic and process until the whole mixture is a thick paste. Cook the paste with the spices in the oil for 4 to 5 minutes, until the juices have run from the mushrooms. Add the canned tomatoes and tomato paste and cook for a further 4 to 5 minutes, to reduce the tomato juice.

Transfer the mixture to a large bowl and add the chopped nuts and bread crumbs. Season well with salt and pepper, then bind with the beaten egg. Spoon the mixture into the prepared pan, cover with lightly oiled foil, and bake in the preheated oven for 1 hour, or until set. Remove the foil and cook for a further 10–15 minutes.

Prepare the salsa. Heat a nonstick skillet, add the cumin seeds, and roast for 1 to 2 minutes. Crush lightly in a mortar and pestle. Combine the cumin with all the remaining ingredients and leave the salsa for about 1 hour. Stir before serving.

Wild Rice Casserole

Serves 4

This recipe was given to me by my friend Jane, who hails from Minnesota, one of the principal wild rice growing areas of the U.S. Wild rice is still something of a luxury for many of us, being very expensive to harvest in the traditional way— from swamp boats. It is not really a rice—more a grass seed—but that does not sound gastronomically correct! A cultivated wild rice (how wild is that?) is now available, more reasonably priced. Luckily, Jane's aunt is still mailing regular supplies, of which I am a grateful beneficiary.

1 Tbsp butter
1 Tbsp olive oil
1 onion, chopped finely
1 red bell pepper, chopped
2 cups chopped mushrooms
1 cup pecan nuts, chopped roughly
1 cup wild rice
3 cups well-flavored chicken or vegetable broth
¼ cup freshly chopped parsley
Salt and freshly ground black pepper
Freshly chopped parsley to garnish

Preheat an oven to 325°F. Heat the butter and oil together in a large flameproof casserole, then add the onion and pepper and cook slowly for about 5 minutes. Stir in the mushrooms and pecans and continue cooking until the juices run from the mushrooms, then add the wild rice. Stir well, then pour in the broth.

Bring the casserole to a boil then add the parsley. Cover and bake in the preheated oven for 1¼ –1½ hours, until the rice has absorbed practically all the broth. Season to taste, then serve with a green salad.

Wild Rice Casserole ▶

Peanut and Bean Sprout Risotto

Serves 4

I have served this dish countless times to vegetarian friends, always with great success. I like to use dry-roasted jumbo peanuts, which add a delicious crunch to the risotto.

- 1½ cups brown rice
- 1 large onion, sliced finely
- 2 Tbsps olive oil
- 1 red bell pepper, seeded and sliced
- 1½ cups sliced mushrooms
- 3 Tbsps soy sauce
- 4 hard-boiled eggs
- 2 handfuls bean sprouts
- 1 cup dry-roasted jumbo peanuts
- 1–2 Tbsps roughly chopped cilantro
- Salt and freshly ground black pepper

Bring the rice to a boil in a large pan of water, then simmer for 35–40 minutes, until tender. Drain well.

Cook the onion in the oil in a large skillet until softened but not browned. Add the pepper and cook for 1 to 2 minutes before adding the rice and mushrooms. Season with the soy sauce and stir-fry for 3 to 4 minutes, until the mushrooms are cooked and the rice has heated through.

Chop 3 of the hard-boiled eggs and add them to the pan with the bean sprouts and peanuts. Season the risotto with salt and pepper if necessary, then continue cooking for a further 1 to 2 minutes before adding the cilantro. Slice the remaining egg and use to garnish the risotto just before serving.

Curried Lentil Soufflé

Serves 3

Lentils are an unusual base for a soufflé and curry is an unusual flavoring, but both work well in this excellent lunch or supper dish. Serve with a simple fresh salad.

- ⅔ cup red lentils
- 1–2 tsps curry powder
- 1½ cups broth or water
- 2 Tbsps butter
- 1 Tbsp fine whole-wheat flour
- ⅔ cup milk
- 1 Tbsp Dijon or yellow mustard
- 3 large eggs, separated
- Salt and freshly ground black pepper

Preheat oven to 350°F and lightly grease a 6 to 7-inch soufflé dish. Bring the lentils, curry powder, and water to a boil in a pan, then simmer for 10–15 minutes until the lentils have softened and cooked into a thick purée. Beat well, then transfer to a bowl to cool slightly.

Melt the butter in the same pan, then stir in the flour. Cook slowly for 1 minute, then gradually add the milk. Bring to a boil, stirring all the time, then cook until very thick. Add the mustard, egg yolks, and lentils and blend well. Season lightly with salt and pepper.

Whisk the egg whites until stiff, then fold them into the lentil mixture. Turn into the prepared dish. Bake in the preheated oven for 30–40 minutes, until set. Serve immediately.

◀ Peanut and Bean Sprout Risotto

Thai-style Beef

Serves 4

Beef marries well with the strong flavors of garlic, oyster sauce, and lemon grass. This dish is unusual as it combines potatoes with a stir-fry—you could use rice or noodles if you prefer.

- 5–6 cups small new potatoes in their skins
- 3 Tbsps corn oil
- 8 thin slices topside of beef, cut into strips
- 3 cups broccoli florets and stalks, chopped roughly
- ⅔ cup scallions, chopped roughly
- 2 cups sliced mushrooms
- 1 piece lemon grass, trimmed and sliced
- 2 cloves garlic, sliced finely
- 1 cup salted cashew nuts
- ½ cup oyster sauce
- ¼ cup water
- ½ cup cilantro leaves

Bring the potatoes to a boil in a pan of water, then simmer for 10 minutes. Drain and leave until cool enough to handle, then slice in half lengthways.

Heat the oil in a large wok or skillet, then add the beef and stir-fry for 1 minute. Add the prepared vegetables with the lemon grass and garlic, and continue cooking for a further 3–4 minutes. Stir the potatoes into the pan with the cashews, oyster sauce, and water, then cook for a further 1–2 minutes until the sauce is bubbling. Add the cilantro leaves immediately before serving.

Apple Ratatouille with Spiced Pork

Serves 4

I have always been keen on recipes which will satisfy meat-eaters and vegetarians alike, and this is one of them. The pork is cooked separately and may be taken only by those who want it. The ratatouille is a meal in itself, but contains cider, apples, and corn, all of which complement the pork well.

Marinade
- ¼ cup black bean or hoi-sin sauce
- 2 tsps Thai 7-Spice seasoning
- 2 Tbsps soy sauce
- 12 oz pork fillet or tenderloin, in one thick piece if possible

- ½ cup black beans, soaked overnight
- 1 large onion, sliced finely
- 3 Tbsps oil
- 2–3 plump cloves garlic, sliced finely
- 1 small eggplant, sliced
- 1 green bell pepper, seeded and sliced
- 1 cup baby corn, halved
- 1 large tart green apple, peeled, cored and sliced
- 14-oz can chopped tomatoes
- 1 cup dry cider
- Salt and freshly ground black pepper

Mix together the ingredients for the marinade, then add the pork and coat thoroughly with the mixture. Leave to stand for at least 1 hour, turning the pork once or twice.

Drain the beans and rinse them thoroughly under cold running water. Bring to a boil in a pan of fresh water then cover and simmer gently until required.

Preheat an oven to 400°F. Transfer the pork to a small roasting pan and spoon the marinade over. Roast in the preheated oven for 30 minutes. Meanwhile, cook the onion in the oil in a large pan until softened but not browned, then add the remaining ratatouille vegetables, the apple, and the cider. Drain the beans, add them to the pan, then bring to a boil. Simmer for about 20 minutes, until the beans and the vegetables are tender.

Slice the pork thinly and serve it with the ratatouille. Serve with baked or mashed potatoes.

main dishes

Apple Ratatouille with Spiced Pork

Spiced Lamb with Garbanzo Beans

Serves 6

Heavy with Middle Eastern flavors, this spicy stew is made with lean lamb fillet mixed with garbanzo beans, pistachios, and apricots.

½ cup garbanzo beans, soaked overnight
8 oz lamb neck fillet, sliced
3 Tbsps olive oil
1 onion, sliced finely
1 small eggplant, sliced finely
2 tsps ground cumin
1 tsp ground allspice
1 cinnamon stick, broken
⅔ cup red wine
14-oz can chopped tomatoes
1 cup well-flavored broth
½ cup dried apricots
Salt and freshly ground black pepper
2 cups couscous
⅓ cup pistachio kernels
Olive oil
Freshly chopped parsley

Drain the garbanzo beans and rinse thoroughly. Bring to a boil in a pan of fresh water then cover and simmer for 30–40 minutes.

Fry the meat in the oil until browned on all sides, then remove the meat from the pan with a slotted spoon and set aside until needed. Add the onion and eggplant to the oil and cook over a high heat until golden brown, adding a little extra oil if necessary. Stir in the spices and continue cooking over a very low heat for 1 to 2 minutes.

Return the lamb fillet to the pan and add the wine. Bring to a boil then simmer until well reduced, scraping up any sediment from the bottom of the pan. Stir in the tomatoes, broth, and apricots and add a little seasoning. Add the drained beans, cover and simmer for 30 minutes.

After 20 minutes, pour a little warm water over the couscous and leave for 10 minutes. Transfer to a steamer. Stir the nuts into the stew; place the couscous over the pan and cover. Cook for 15–20 minutes.

Dress the couscous with olive oil and season it lightly. Season the stew and serve on a bed of couscous. Garnish with parsley.

Lamb with Lentils and Prunes

Serves 4

This casserole has many of the classic flavors of southwest France: plump, moist prunes, green lentils, and fresh thyme. The lentils and prunes make it a filling dish and mean that much less meat is required per person than in a more traditional casserole.

1 Tbsp olive oil
1 Tbsp butter
4 lamb chops or leg steaks, or 1 pound lamb fillet, cut into 4 pieces
1 large onion, sliced
3 sticks celery, sliced
2 large carrots, sliced
2 plump cloves garlic, sliced finely
1 Tbsp fine whole-wheat flour
2 cups well-flavored vegetable or lamb broth
1 cup prunes
½ cup green lentils
6 juniper berries, lightly crushed
4–5 sprigs fresh thyme
Salt and freshly ground black pepper

Preheat an oven to 325°F. Heat the oil and butter together in a flameproof casserole dish and brown the lamb on all sides. Remove the meat with a slotted spoon and set aside until needed. Add the onion to the casserole and cook slowly until softened but not browned, then add the celery, carrot, and garlic and continue cooking for a further 2 to 3 minutes.

Stir the flour into the vegetables and cook for 1 to 2 minutes, then gradually add the broth, stirring to scrape up any sediment from the bottom of the pan. Bring to a boil; add the prunes and lentils and simmer for 2 to 3 minutes. Return the lamb to the casserole and add the remaining seasonings. Cover, then cook in the preheated oven for 1½–2 hours. Season to taste before serving the lamb on a bed of the vegetables with the sauce spooned over.

Lamb with Lentils and Prunes ▶

Spiced Cod Cobbler

Serves 4

Fish is a very healthy diet food, most varieties being low in fat. It is not always easy, however, to know how to incorporate fish into a high-fiber meal—I think a cobbler topping is the answer.

2 cups sliced button mushrooms
1½ pounds thick cod fillet, skinned
4 tomatoes, halved
1 Tbsp butter
Salt and freshly ground black pepper

Topping
1½ cups fresh whole-wheat bread crumbs
1 small onion, chopped very finely
Salt and freshly ground black pepper
2 Tbsps sunflower oil

Preheat oven to 375°F. Make a layer of the mushrooms in the bottom of an ovenproof dish. Cut the cod into four pieces and arrange them over the mushrooms. Place the tomatoes around the edge of the dish. Cut the butter into slivers and dot them over the fish, then season lightly with salt and pepper.

Blend the bread crumbs with the onion and seasonings. Pour in the oil and mix lightly, then spread the crumbs over the fish. Bake in the preheated oven for 30 minutes, until the topping is crisp and the fish is cooked. Serve with fresh green vegetables.

Spanish-Style Haddock

Serves 4

This traditional Spanish dish of haddock is very similar to Mexican dishes where cod or other firm, white-fleshed fish are marinated in lime juice. This is not so highly spiced as a Mexican dish would be, and the lightly cooked vegetables add plenty of fiber. Serve with whole-wheat bread to mop up the juices.

1 pound thick haddock fillet or similar white fish, skinned
3 Tbsps fruity olive oil
1 mild onion, sliced finely
2 plump cloves garlic, sliced finely
1 cup sliced button mushrooms
1 red bell pepper, seeded and sliced
1 green bell pepper, seeded and sliced
Salt and freshly ground black pepper
½ cup white wine vinegar
⅓ cup water
1 Tbsp white sugar

Cut the fish into bite-sized pieces. Heat two tablespoons of the oil in a skillet and fry the fish until just cooked. Transfer it to a glass or china dish. Heat the remaining oil in the skillet; add the onion and garlic and cook until soft but not browned. Stir in the mushrooms and peppers and cook for a further 1 to 2 minutes—the vegetables should retain a crisp texture. Spoon the vegetables over the fish and season lightly.

Pour the vinegar and water into the skillet and bring to a boil. Stir in the sugar until dissolved, then pour the liquid over the fish and vegetables. Leave to cool, then cover and place in the refrigerator for 24 hours. Serve for a summer lunch or supper dish with whole-wheat bread.

▲ Spanish-Style Haddock

Stir-fried Trout

Serves 2–3

I always find it difficult to devise high-fiber fish recipes, but this one works very well. Crispy stir-fried vegetables contrast well with the soft texture of the fish—it is even better if the trout is freshly caught.

3 Tbsps oil
4 cups mixed stir-fry vegetables
1 onion, cut into wedges
1 chile, seeded and chopped
2 large trout fillets, about 1 lb, skinned and cut into 2-inch pieces
7oz-can water chestnuts, drained and halved
2 handfuls bean sprouts
2 Tbsps soy sauce
1 Tbsp chile sauce
Shin joi – hot oriental cress to garnish

Heat the oil in a wok or a large skillet until almost smoking. Add the prepared vegetables, onion, and chile then stir-fry for 1 minute. Add the trout and water chestnuts, and continue cooking over a very high heat for 2–3 minutes, until the fish is almost cooked—don't stir too vigorously or the fish will break up. Finally, add the bean sprouts, soy and chile sauces and cook for a further 1 minute. Serve immediately.

Trout with Wild Rice Stuffing

Serves 4

Wild rice makes excellent stuffings. It goes well with game birds such as pheasant and duck, or with fish. I do not mix the stuffing with egg when I use it with fish, as a crumbly stuffing seems to go better with the flaky fish texture.

Stuffing
1 small onion, chopped finely
1 stalk celery, sliced finely
1 Tbsp oil
½ small green bell pepper, chopped finely
1 clove garlic, crushed
1½ cups cooked wild rice (about ⅓ cup raw)
1 Tbsp freshly chopped dill or parsley
1 lemon, grated rind and juice
Salt and freshly ground black pepper

4 trout, brown or rainbow

Preheat an oven to 400°F. Lightly butter a suitable ovenproof dish.

Cook the onion and celery in the oil until softened but not browned. Add the pepper and continue cooking until all the vegetables are soft. Remove the pan from the heat and stir in the garlic and cooked rice. Add the herbs, lemon rind, and juice, then season to taste with salt and freshly ground black pepper.

Clean the trout, removing the heads if preferred. Season the cavities lightly and fill with the stuffing. Arrange the fish in the prepared dish and cover with foil. Bake for 15–20 minutes, according to the size of the fish, until just cooked. Serve immediately while still hot.

Trout with Wild Rice Stuffing ▶

desserts

I know that I am not alone in either missing out completely on desserts during the week, or just having a piece of fresh fruit or a bowl of yogurt. However, when time allows, dessert is the perfect ending to a good meal, a treat to be thoroughly enjoyed.

Many of the desserts included here contain fruit. Berries and exotic fruits, such as mangoes, are best eaten in a simple fruit salad, especially if they are fully ripened, but using just a few fruits rather than filling a bowl with numerous varieties can produce a stylish, light dessert; for example, strawberries served with melon and orange. Make a change by serving a flavored, blended cream instead of heavy cream—lime marscapone is perfect with a dish of peaches and raspberries.

Red and black currants are expensive to buy, even when they are in season, as they are time consuming to pick and have a very short shelf life. I usually buy them frozen in fruit mixes; then they are reasonably priced and make a wonderful base for any number of desserts.

Beans are not usually the first choice of ingredients for a dessert, but adzuki beans, which are semi-sweet, are good in both savory and sweet dishes. The Sweet Bean & Apple Cobbler that I have included here is delicious and I thoroughly recommend it. Although white rice does not contain as much fiber as brown, it is still a source of fiber and should not be disregarded in a high-fiber diet. I am a rice pudding addict and have included an everyday rice pudding, as well as a much creamier pudding with fresh mangoes and grapes stirred into it.

desserts

Plum and Apple Pudding

Serves 4–6

When the weather is cold, you can't beat a traditional pudding with a sponge topping. I like to use a mixture of apples and plums, and to flavor the dish lightly with ginger. The sponge layer is very thin in this pudding, so it is not too filling.

2 pounds tart green apples and plums, mixed
¼ cup light brown sugar

Topping
½ cup margarine
½ cup light brown sugar
1 large egg, beaten
1¼ cups fine whole-wheat flour
1 tsp baking powder
Pinch of salt
1 tsp ground ginger
1 Tbsp milk

Preheat an oven to 375°F. Peel, core, and slice the apples, then cut the plums in half and remove the stones. Cut the plums into quarters if they are very firm. Mix the fruits and place in a suitable ovenproof dish—I use an 8-inch, round flan dish—then scatter the sugar on top.

Cream the margarine and sugar for the topping together until pale and creamy, then beat in the egg. Mix the flour, baking powder, salt, and ginger together, then fold into the egg mixture with the milk. Spoon the mixture as evenly as possible over the fruits. Bake in the preheated oven for about 30–35 minutes, until the sponge is set and shrinking slightly from the sides of the dish. Serve hot.

Apricot Cheesecake

Serves 8–10

To avoid the disappointment of mixtures not setting, I never keep gelatin for longer than 6 months. Always check the "sell-by" date on the packet carefully—old gelatin simply will not work. This recipe contains uncooked egg white.

1½ cups dried apricots
1½ cups water
1 cup lowfat cream cheese, or strained cottage cheese
1 cup thick plain yogurt
1 Tbsp powdered gelatin
2 large egg whites
Fine strips of orange rind

Base
¼ cup butter
¼ cup honey
2 cups granola

Soak the apricots in the water for 4 hours.

Melt the butter in a pan, then stir in the honey and granola; mix well. Press the mixture into the base of a deep, 8-inch, spring-form or loose-bottomed cake pan—use the back of a metal spoon to level the mixture. Chill until required.

Reserve ⅓ cup of liquid from the apricots. Purée the fruit with the remaining juice in a blender or food processor until smooth—add a little extra water if necessary to achieve a smooth paste. Turn into a bowl and beat in the cheese and yogurt.

Heat the reserved apricot juice until almost at a boil in a small pan, then remove from the heat and sprinkle the gelatin over. Stir until almost dissolved then leave to stand for 2 minutes, until completely dissolved. Stir one heaping tablespoon of the apricot mixture into the gelatin—this helps to incorporate it evenly—then fold the gelatin into the apricot mixture. Whisk the egg whites until stiff, then fold them into the apricots.

Pour the mixture over the granola base and smooth the top. Chill in the refrigerator for 2 to 3 hours until set. Carefully remove the cheesecake from the pan and decorate with fine strips of orange rind just before serving.

▲ Apricot Cheesecake

Spiced Berry Pudding

Serves 8

I first thought of this pudding when I wanted a fresh, fruity alternative to the traditional Christmas pudding. It is based on a classic summer pudding, but the berries are spiced and I use a fruit bread. The result is a perfect blend of seasonal flavors. I always use frozen fruits because they are so much cheaper than fresh.

desserts

1½ pounds mixed berries, e.g., raspberries, blueberries, strawberries, and currants, fresh or frozen
¾ cup light brown sugar
1 teaspoon ground cinnamon
1 small fruit loaf, unsliced

Cook the berries with the sugar and cinnamon until they start to burst, then remove from the heat and set to one side.

Remove the crusts from the bread and cut it into quarter-inch slices. Arrange the slices in a suitable pudding mold, cutting them so that they fit the mold neatly. Remove the bread and dip it, on both sides, in the fruit juices, then return it to the mold. Add the berries, removing them from the pan with a slotted spoon. Add sufficient juice to almost cover the berries (the bread will absorb a little more juice) then cover the pudding with more bread, dipping the slices into the juices.

Cover the pudding with a plate or saucer that will just sit on top of the bread, then place some heavy weights or cans on the plate. Allow the pudding to cool, then chill it for at least 6 hours or overnight.

To serve, turn the pudding out of the basin carefully—providing that it has been well weighted and properly chilled, it should turn out easily and keep its shape. Serve with any remaining juices and yogurt or cream.

◀ Spiced Berry Pudding

Sweet Fruits Pilau

Serves 4

I am a rice pudding addict and, although I am very fond of the basic pudding served simply with a spoonful of jam, I also enjoy dressing the recipe up, to turn it into something special. This recipe combines the basic pudding with ripe tropical fruits. Serve it warm—it's delicious. Add chopped toasted nuts at the end of cooking if you wish, but I prefer the pudding without, as all the textures of the fruits and the rice are then similar.

1/3 cup pudding rice
1 Tbsp light brown sugar
6 cloves
2 bay leaves
2 cups milk
1 cup light cream
1 orange
1 ripe mango, roughly chopped
2/3 cup seedless grapes, halved

Preheat an oven to 300°F. Place the rice in a large ovenproof dish with the sugar and spices, then add the milk and cream. Stir briefly then bake in the preheated oven for 2 hours. The rice will be creamier and wetter than for a traditional rice pudding.

Remove the skin and spices from the pudding then leave for 20 minutes to cool. Meanwhile, prepare the fruits. Grate the rind from the orange and reserve it for decoration, then peel the fruit and chop the flesh roughly. Mix the orange with the mango and grapes, then stir the fruits into the warm rice. Serve immediately.

Fresh Apricots with Dried Cherries and Ginger

Serves 4

I think I really prefer dried apricots—the intensity of flavor is so much stronger. However, when the ripe fruits are in the shops I like to draw out their sweetness by adding dried cherries and stem ginger in syrup. I add a little freshly chopped pineapple mint when it is available in the garden.

8 large apricots
1/3 cup semi-dried cherries, chopped roughly
4 pieces preserved ginger, chopped finely
4 Tbsps ginger syrup

Cut the apricots in half and remove the pits—cut the fruits into quarters if they are very large. Add the chopped cherries and ginger to the apricots with the syrup from the ginger and stir gently to coat all the fruits. Chill for no more than 45 minutes before serving.

Warm Spiced Compote

Serves 6

Apple rings, pears, peaches, and cranberries are now widely available dried, as are prunes, apricots, and figs. I have never been very keen on compote made just from apricots and prunes, but when they are mixed with some of the milder fruits the dish takes on a new dimension.

2 cups roughly chopped mixed dried fruits
1 cup water
1½ cups orange juice
3 green cardamoms
1 cinnamon stick, broken

Thick plain yogurt
⅓ cup roughly chopped brazil nuts

Place the fruits in a small pan with the water and orange juice. Crush the cardamom pods and discard the husks. Crush the seeds lightly, then add them to the fruit with the cinnamon stick. Heat gently until almost at a boil, then remove the pan from the heat, cover, and leave to stand for 3 to 4 hours.

Remove the cinnamon stick and reheat the fruits gently before serving, topped with yogurt and chopped brazil nuts.

Banana and Rhubarb Trifle

Serves 6

Bananas and rhubarb are a wonderful combination of fruits for cobblers, pies and trifles. I toss the banana slices in lime juice, which not only stops them browning but also brings out the flavor of the rhubarb—a tip I picked up on vacation in Iceland.

    2 cups cooked rhubarb pieces, fresh or canned
    2 cups sliced banana
    ½ cup rhubarb juice or syrup
    Grated rind and juice of 1 lime
    2 pieces preserved ginger, chopped finely
    ¼ cup honey
    1 cup thick plain yogurt
    ¼ cup wheat germ

Purée the rhubarb, banana, rhubarb juice, lime rind, and juice in a blender or food processor. Turn into a bowl and add the ginger with honey to taste. Fold the yogurt into the mixture with the wheat germ, then cover and chill for 1 to 2 hours. Serve decorated with a little extra wheat germ.

Atholl Brose

Serves 6–8

Atholl Brose used to be served as a drink, but these days it is more usual to have it as a dessert. It is a traditional Scottish dish of oatmeal, cream, and honey, and it is utterly addictive—and, of course, with orange juice and oatmeal in it, it *must* be good for you!

    ⅓ cup oatmeal
    1½ cups heavy cream
    ½ cup light cream
    2–3 Tbsps honey
    ¼ cup whiskey
    Grated rind and juice of 1 orange

Toast the oatmeal until golden brown, either in a hot, dry skillet or under a preheated broiler. Allow to cool.

Whisk the creams together until thick and floppy but not stiff. Add the honey, whiskey, and orange juice and whisk briefly until they are evenly incorporated into the cream. Fold in the oatmeal and orange rind, then turn into a serving bowl and chill lightly before serving.

desserts

◄ Banana and Rhubarb Trifle

Prune and Walnut Tart

Serves 6

Baked in crisp pastry and made with cream for a special occasion. One mouthful of this tart and I am in prune country in southwest France or California, soaking up the sunshine and planning the next trip to the local vineyard. . . .

Pastry
½ cup butter
1¼ cups fine whole-wheat flour
1 Tbsp light brown sugar
1 large egg, beaten

Filling
2 Tbsps plum jam or apple jelly
⅔ cup pitted prunes, chopped roughly
⅓ cup walnut pieces, chopped roughly
1¼ cups milk or light cream
2 large eggs, beaten
1 tsp superfine sugar (optional)
Freshly grated nutmeg

Prepare the pastry by blending the butter into the flour and sugar. Bind together with the beaten egg then knead gently on a lightly floured surface. Cover the pastry with plastic wrap and chill in a refrigerator for 30 minutes.

Preheat an oven to 400°F. Roll out the pastry to line a deep, 8-inch flan or cake pan, preferably with a loose base. Fill the pastry case with baking parchment and baking beans, then bake for 15 minutes. Remove the baking beans and parchment and continue cooking for a further five minutes, until the base is dry.

Reduce the oven heat to 350°F. Spread the jam over the base of the flan case then top with the prunes and walnuts. Beat the milk or cream with the eggs and sugar, if used, then pour the custard into the flan case and grate some nutmeg over the top. Bake for 40 minutes, or until the custard is lightly set. Allow to cool, then serve warm or cold.

Prune and Brandy Mousse

Serves 6

Whenever I vacation in southwest France, I always return with several jars of prune purée—it is wonderful in ice cream, with pheasant, and in pies. Here, I have made my own purée, which is combined with cream and egg whites to make a light mousse. This recipe contains uncooked egg white.

1 cup pitted prunes
½ cup brandy, or orange juice and brandy mixed
1–2 Tbsps light brown sugar
1 cup heavy cream
1 cup light cream
2 large egg whites

Purée the prunes with the brandy in a blender or food processor until smooth, then sweeten to taste with the sugar.

Whip the creams together until soft and floppy—do not beat until stiff—then fold the cream into the prune purée. Whisk the egg whites until stiff; fold them into the prune cream. Turn into 1 large bowl or 6 individual glasses and chill lightly before serving.

Prune and Walnut Tart ▶

Brown Bread Ice Cream

Serves 6–8

Brown bread ice cream was a popular dessert in Victorian times and has recently enjoyed a great revival. It is not as sweet as many frozen desserts. The most important tip for success is to have the bread crumbs completely dry before adding them to the mixture, or they will become soggy in the ice cream.

2 cups milk
1 vanilla bean
4 egg yolks
½ cup light brown sugar
⅔ cup heavy cream
1 cup whole-wheat bread crumbs, evenly toasted

Heat the milk with the vanilla bean until almost at a boil, then leave to stand for 10 minutes before removing the vanilla. Beat the egg yolks with the sugar until a thick paste. Return the milk to the heat and bring almost to simmering point, then pour onto the egg yolks in a steady stream, beating all the time. Rinse the pan, return the custard to it, and heat gently, stirring until the mixture will coat the back of a wooden spoon. Do not be tempted to overcook the custard or it will curdle. Turn the custard into a bowl and allow it to cool completely.

Chill the custard in a freezer for 1½ hours, until thick and slushy. Whip the cream until soft and floppy. Fold it into the custard with the bread crumbs, then return the ice cream to the freezer. Stir after 1 hour, then leave for a further 2 to 3 hours until completely set.

Remove the ice cream from the freezer about 30 minutes before serving, to allow it to soften.

Fig and Pecan Pie

Serves 8

Pecan pie is a vital part of the traditional Thanksgiving dinner. I like this variation on the traditional theme—the figs add an extra texture to the pie without making it too sweet.

Pastry
1 stick butter
1½ cups fine whole-wheat flour
Pinch of salt
Warm water

Filling
1 stick unsalted butter
⅓ cup light brown sugar
½ cup honey
2 tsps vanilla
1 Tbsp coffee essence
¼ cup whiskey or orange juice
1 cup figs, chopped roughly
2 cups pecan halves

Preheat an oven to 375°F. Prepare the pastry by blending the butter into the flour and salt. Add sufficient warm water to make a firm dough, then roll out and use to line a 10-inch, loose-bottomed flan case. Chill in the refrigerator while preparing the filling.

Cream the butter and sugar together until pale and creamy, then beat in the honey and vanilla. Add the coffee essence and the whiskey; beat in the figs and half the pecans, chopped. The mixture will appear to curdle, but don't worry!

Place the pastry case on a cookie sheet, then spread the pastry with the filling. Arrange the remaining pecan nuts on top of the pie. Bake in the preheated oven for 40 minutes. The filling will bubble up through the nuts during cooking, giving them a crunchy coating. Serve the pie warm or cold, with ice cream or yogurt.

Strawberries with Melon and Orange

Serve 4

Strawberries and other berry fruits are a good source of fiber, whereas melons—containing so much water and with an inedible skin—are not so fiber rich. Mix them together and you have a good combination of flavors and textures, as well as a colorful dessert. Remove the membrane from the orange segments if you prefer.

3 cups halved strawberries
1 small Galia melon, balled
2 oranges
¼ cup orange juice (optional)
Mint leaves

Place the halved strawberries in a bowl with the melon balls. Peel the oranges and break into segments, then cut them in half or chop them roughly, depending on size. Add the oranges to the other fruits with any juices, adding extra orange juice if necessary. The fruits will usually create their own juice, especially if the melon is ripe. Leave to stand for 30 minutes. Serve the fruit salad at room temperature, decorated with the fresh mint leaves.

Spiced Honeyed Gooseberries

Serves 4

My gooseberry bush is under an elder tree and as soon as the flowers are fully out, I know that the gooseberries will be ripe. Use a combination of elderflowers and saffron, or just one or the other.

    4 cups gooseberries, topped and tailed
    ⅓ cup honey
    Pinch of saffron strands (optional)
    2–3 heads elderflowers, or 1 Tbsp elderflower
      cordial (optional)
    2–3 Tbsps Demerara sugar

Mix the gooseberries with the honey and chosen flavorings in a small pan. Cover and cook over a very low heat for 10–15 minutes, until just softened and ready to split. Remove the elderflowers, if used, and pour the gooseberries into a well-buttered oven proof dish.

Preheat a broiler. Scatter the Demerara sugar over the fruit and cook under the broiler until it has melted and caramelized. Serve hot or cold.

Mango Yogurt Brulée

Serves 4

Crème brulée is one of my all-time favorite puddings, especially when made with thick cream. This recipe is slightly healthier, but still delicious.

    1 large ripe mango
    1½ cups thick plain yogurt
    3 Tbsps All-Bran cereal, crushed
    ½ cup raw sugar

Peel the mango, remove the stone, and chop the flesh, then divide it between four ovenproof ramekin dishes.

Preheat a broiler. Blend the yogurt with the cereal, breaking the strands into smaller pieces, then spoon it over the fruit. Spoon a thick layer of sugar over the yogurt, so that it is covered.

Cook the puddings under the hot broiler for 1 to 2 minutes, until the sugar has melted. Do not overcook, or the yogurt will bubble up through the sugar. Allow to cool, then chill for at least 1 hour before serving.

Pineapple with Apricots and Berries

Serves 4

A ripe pineapple really should be eaten just on its own, with no extra gilding. This can, however, seem like a lack of effort when entertaining, so here is an unusual combination of fresh and dried fruits to grace any dinner table.

    ½ cup dried or ready-to-eat apricots, soaked if
      necessary
    1 large ripe pineapple
    1 cup raspberries
    1 cup blueberries
    Sugar to taste

Chop the apricots roughly. Cut the pineapple in half lengthways if you wish to use it for serving, and cut away the flesh to leave a firm shell. Alternatively, peel the pineapple, core it and dice the flesh into large chunks.

Mix the prepared pineapple with the apricots, raspberries, and blueberries, adding sugar as necessary, then pile the fruit into the prepared shell or a serving dish. Chill lightly before serving.

desserts

Carrot Pudding

Serves 3–4

Young carrots have a very sweet flavor and it is not a new idea to use them in a pudding—they have traditionally been baked and steamed in many countries in rich fruit puddings. The younger the carrots, the better. This would be a good dish to serve after a hot curry or a spicy chili.

    1½ cups milk
    3 green cardamoms, crushed
    1 cinnamon stick, broken
    6 cloves
    1 cup grated carrot
    ¼ cup pistachio kernels
    ⅓ cup chopped pitted dates
    1 tsp light brown sugar
    3 large eggs, beaten

Heat the milk with the spices until almost at a boil, then leave to stand for 20 minutes before straining. Preheat an oven to 325°F.

Place the carrot, pistachios, and dates in a lightly greased pie dish. Beat the sugar with the eggs, then add the strained milk. Pour the mixture over the carrots, stir briefly, then bake in the preheated oven for about 1½ hours, or until set. Serve warm with a sweet cookie such as shortbread.

Apricot Bread and Butter Pudding

Serves 4

This pudding is usually made with currants and raisins but I prefer it with apricots. I also tuck all the fruit inside the pudding so that it will not burn and turn bitter during cooking.

    3–4 slices whole-wheat bread
    Margarine or butter
    ½ cup roughly chopped dried apricots
    ¼ cup golden raisins
    2 cups milk
    3 large eggs
    1 Tbsp light brown sugar

Preheat an oven to 350°F. Butter the bread and cut it into triangular quarters. Arrange half the bread in the bottom of a large pie dish. Scatter the dried fruits over, then top with the remaining bread. Beat the milk with the eggs and sugar then pour over the pudding—if you leave the crusts on the bread, I suggest leaving the pudding to stand for 15-20 minutes before cooking, to allow the crusts to soften.

Bake the pudding for 35–40 minutes, until the custard is set. Serve warm, not hot.

Sweet Bean and Apple Cobbler

Serves 6

Adzuki beans have a slightly sweet flavor and are used in both savory and sweet dishes. I hope you like this cobbler—I think it is delicious but I was very sceptical about beans in a dessert before I tried it! The Chinese have been making sweet bean puddings for centuries.

⅓ cup adzuki beans, soaked overnight
½ tsp ground cinnamon
¼ cup honey
2 cups finely sliced tart green apples

Crumble
⅓ cup butter
1 cup whole-wheat flour
½ cup All-Bran cereal
1 Tbsp light brown sugar

Drain the adzuki beans, then rinse them under cold running water. Bring to a boil in a pan of fresh water, then cover and simmer for 30 minutes or until tender. Drain and set to one side.

Preheat oven to 375°F. Combine the cinnamon and honey and mix into the apples and adzuki beans in a suitable ovenproof dish. Blend the butter into the flour, All-Bran, and sugar, then spoon the cobbler mixture over the fruit. Bake in the preheated oven for 30–35 minutes, until the cobbler has browned and set. Serve with custard, cream, or yogurt.

Sweet Bean and Apple Cobbler ▶

Apple and Pecan Mincemeat

Makes approximately 3 pounds

Mincemeat is a mixture of dried fruits, suet, sugar, and alcohol—or that is what it should be! I always try to make my own mincemeat at Christmas because it has a firmer, more distinctive texture— as well as a much better flavor—than any of the commercial varieties.

  1 pound tart green apples, peeled, cored, and
    sliced
  1 cup golden raisins
  1 cup seedless raisins
  1 cup finely chopped dried apricots
  1 cup pecans, chopped roughly
  1 cup light brown sugar
  Grated rind and juice of 1 orange
  1 tsp ground cinnamon
  1 nutmeg, freshly ground, or 1 tsp ground
  1 tsp ground cloves
  1 cup shredded suet
  ¼ cup whiskey

Cook the apples to a pulp with as little water as possible—I like to use the microwave for this because no water at all is required. Beat the apples thoroughly, then leave them until completely cold.

Stir all the remaining ingredients into the apples, adding the suet and whiskey last. Cover and leave overnight to allow the flavors to blend.

Stir the mincemeat again, then spoon it into warm, clean jars. Cover and seal, then store in a cool place for at least 3 weeks before using in pies, tarts, or as a filling for baked apples.

Mincemeat and Apple Tart

Serves 6

Mincemeat is full of fiber from the dried fruits that it contains. I like to make it into a tart with apples, which take away much of the richness— mixing the pastry with a little orange rind and juice also helps.

Pastry
⅓ cup butter
1 cup fine whole-wheat flour
Grated rind and juice of 1 orange

2 cups mincemeat
1–2 sweet red-skinned apples, cored and sliced
Juice of 1 lemon
2 Tbsps honey

Preheat an oven to 375°F. Blend the butter into the flour, then stir in the orange rind. Bind the pastry together with the orange juice, then roll it out and use to line an 8-inch cake or flan pan.

Spread the mincemeat evenly in the pastry case then arrange the sliced apples around the edge, brushing them with lemon juice. Bake the tart in the preheated oven for 30–35 minutes.

Brush the apples carefully with honey as soon as the tart is removed from the oven, then leave to cool slightly before serving.

Mincemeat and Apple Tart ▶

Rum and Raisin Yogurt Ice Cream

Serves 6–8

This is my favorite method for making ice cream —it requires no stirring during freezing and produces a dessert which is full of body but not too rich. I find that some ice creams are rather watery, even when made of the best ingredients.

½ cup seedless raisins
¼ cup rum
2 large egg whites
½ cup light brown sugar
⅓ cup water
⅔ cup thick plain yogurt
1¼ cups heavy cream

Soak the raisins in the rum for 20 minutes before beginning the ice cream.

Whisk the egg whites until stiff. At the same time, heat the sugar with the water until the sugar has dissolved, then bring the syrup to a boil and boil rapidly for 3 minutes. Pour the sugar syrup in a continuous stream onto the whisked egg whites and continue beating for about one minute. Add the yogurt and continue whisking until the mixture is cool; this is best done in a mixer.

Whisk the cream until thick and floppy but not stiff. Drain the raisins and fold the rum into the yogurt mixture, add the cream, and, finally, fold in the raisins. Turn the mixture into a bombe mould or a suitable container and freeze for about 4 hours, until firm. Remove from the freezer 20 minutes before required, to allow it to soften.

Banana Bran Custard

Serves 4

Banana custard has long been a favorite, and this is a variation on the traditional recipe. It is quick to make to serve immediately, but it will keep well in the refrigerator for 2 or 3 days.

1 cup banana slices (2 medium fruits)
Grated rind and juice of 1 lemon
⅔ cup sour cream or yogurt
⅓ cup pecans, chopped roughly
1 Tbsp honey
¼ cup bran
Milk

Toss the banana slices in lemon juice, then place them in a bowl and carefully mix in the cream or yogurt, nuts, honey, and bran. If the mixture is very thick, add 1 or 2 tablespoons of milk to thin it down. Decorate with the lemon rind just before serving. If serving immediately, the honey may be drizzled over the cream in a zigzag pattern.

Banana Bran Custard ▶

▲ Date and Ginger Pudding

Date and Ginger Pudding

Serves 6–8

A favorite winter pudding, sweetened with dates and banana. On a totally decadent day, you could serve this with a toffee or butterscotch sauce, but custard or ice cream would show a modicum of restraint! It could also be sliced when cold and served as a cake.

⅓ cup stoned dates, chopped roughly
2 pieces preserved ginger, chopped finely
1 banana, mashed
2 Tbsps syrup from the ginger

½ cup margarine or butter
½ cup light brown sugar
2 large eggs, beaten
1½ cups fine whole-wheat flour
1½ tsps baking powder
Pinch of salt
2 Tbsps milk

Preheat an oven to 375°F, then lightly grease and line a deep, 7-inch cake pan.

Mix together the dates, ginger, banana, and ginger syrup. Cream the margarine and sugar together until pale and creamy, then beat in the eggs a little at a time. Mix together the flour, baking powder, and salt, then fold them into the mixture. Fold in the date and banana mix, then add a little milk to give a soft, dropping consistency.

Turn into the prepared pan and smooth the top. Bake in the preheated oven for 30–35 minutes, until a toothpick inserted into the center comes out clean, and the pudding shrinks away from the sides of the tin. Serve cut into wedges.

Summer Fruits Upside-Down Trifle

Serves 6–8

This is a very simple trifle, quick to make and delicious to eat. You could use fruit-flavored yogurt, but I prefer to mix the syrup from the berries into plain yogurt to make a well-flavored sauce. The crumbs on the top replace the traditional sponge trifle base.

2 pounds berries, fresh or frozen
1 cup light brown sugar
¼ cup butter
1½ cups crushed Graham crackers
⅔ cup whole almonds, chopped finely
1 cup plain yogurt

Cook the berries with the sugar over a low heat until they just start to burst. Allow the berries to cool, then strain half a cup of syrup from them. Melt the butter, then stir in the Graham cracker crumbs and almonds and mix well. Leave until required. Mix the cooled syrup with the yogurt.

Place the berries in the bottom of a glass serving dish; top with the flavored yogurt. Make a thick layer of the crumbs over the trifle, then chill for at least 30 minutes before serving.

Gooseberry and Orange Trifle

Serves 4

I make gooseberry and orange jam every summer because the flavor combination is outstanding. The combination is just as good in a trifle. Make your own custard if you wish, although I often use prepared custard for speed and convenience.

3 cups gooseberries, topped and tailed
Grated rind and juice of 2 oranges
½ cup raw sugar
1 cup thick custard
1 cup thick plain yogurt
1 Tbsp raw sugar
1 Tbsp bran

Stew the gooseberries with the orange rind, juice, and sugar until soft. Allow the fruit to cool, then fold it into the custard. Blend in the yogurt, either mixing it completely or leaving it marbled through the custard mixture. Spoon into a glass serving bowl or individual dishes and chill for 1 hour.

Mix the remaining tablespoon of sugar with the bran and scatter over the trifle before serving.

Pineapple Oat Meringues

Serves 4

Meringues are so often served with berry fruits, and I like to be different. In this recipe, I have folded toasted oatmeal into the meringue before spooning it over thick slices of fresh pineapple filled with raisins. The result, which is not too sweet, is a wonderful combination of flavors and textures. The raisins could be soaked in a little kirsch or brandy if wished.

2 Tbsps oats
4 slices fresh pineapple, cored
⅓ cup raisins
2 large egg whites
½ cup superfine sugar

Preheat oven to 375°F. Toast the oats until golden brown, either in a hot dry skillet or under a preheated broiler. Leave to cool.

Place the pineapple slices in individual ovenproof dishes and fill the centers with raisins. Whisk the egg whites to stiff peaks, then gradually whisk in the sugar. Fold in the toasted oatmeal, then pile the mixture over the pineapple in the dishes, covering the fruit completely.

Bake in the preheated oven for 5 to 8 minutes, until set and lightly browned. Serve immediately.

Pineapple Oat Meringues ▶

desserts

Orange Rice and Golden Raisin Pudding

Serves 3–4

Rice pudding is one of my favorite desserts—real rib-sticking comfort food! I use orange rind in this pudding to give the rice a light citrus flavor; don't be tempted to add the juice since the pudding will probably curdle.

⅓ cup pudding rice
⅓ cup golden raisins
1 tsp light brown sugar
Grated rind of 1 orange
2 cups milk
Knob of margarine or butter
Freshly grated nutmeg

Preheat an oven to 300°F. Place the rice and raisins in a lightly buttered pie dish then add the sugar and orange rind. Pour in the milk and stir to combine. Dot the top of the pudding with slivers of margarine or butter, then grate some nutmeg over the milk.

Bake the pudding slowly in the preheated oven for 2 hours. Serve hot or cold.

Tangerine and Cream Cheese Pancakes

Makes 8, serves 4

Light pancakes filled with a creamy cheese mixture and chopped fresh tangerines. I love the flavor of orange with whole-wheat pancakes, but other fruits, such as pears and peaches, also work very well.

Filling
½ cup lowfat cream cheese
1 Tbsp light brown sugar
½ cup sour cream
4 tangerines, broken into segments

Batter
1 large egg
1¼ cups milk
1 cup fine whole-wheat flour
Sunflower oil

Beat the cream cheese with the sugar, then blend with the sour cream. Break the tangerines into segments; cut them into halves if they are very big. Set the filling to one side until needed.

Preheat an oven to 375°F. Blend the egg and milk together in a blender or food processor, then add the flour with the motor running. Blend to a smooth batter.

Heat a nonstick skillet until evenly hot, then brush the bottom lightly with oil. Pour a little of the batter into the pan and cook quickly for about 1½ minutes, then turn or flip the pancake over and cook the second side. Stack the cooked pancakes, interleaved in kitchen towels, until all the batter is thoroughly cooked.

Divide the cream cheese mixture between the pancakes, spreading it evenly, then top with the tangerine segments. Roll up the pancakes, or fold them into quarters, and arrange in a large, ovenproof dish. Bake for 10–15 minutes in the preheated oven, just until heated through. Serve immediately while still hot.

desserts

▲ Tangerine and Cream Cheese Pancakes

Danish Apple Cake

Serves 4–6

This pudding was very fashionable a few years ago—I think it is delicious and am spearheading a campaign to revive it! I don't think the apple needs sweetening, but sugar may be added if necessary. You may serve it topped with whipped cream and chocolate . . .

    3 cups fresh whole-wheat bread crumbs
    ⅓ cup raw sugar
    ⅓ cup butter
    4 cups prepared tart green apples, peeled, cored,
       and sliced
    Grated rind and juice of 1 lemon

Mix the bread crumbs with the sugar. Melt the butter in a large skillet, then add the crumb mixture and fry quickly until the crumbs are crisp, then set them to one side.

Cook the apples with the lemon rind and juice and as little water as possible until soft. I usually cook the apples in a microwave because no water at all is required. Allow to cool.

Turn half the apples into a glass dish, then make a layer of half the crumbs over the apples. Repeat the layers, finishing with the remaining crumbs. Allow the pudding to cool completely, then chill for at least 1 hour before serving.

Danish Apple Cake ▶

Fig Baked Apples

Serves 4

I think baked apples are often overlooked simply because they have a relatively long cooking time— about 45 minutes. However, they are very quick to prepare and, if the oven is already on, they can just be popped in the bottom, to cook slowly. If the oven is on at a higher temperature, place the dish of apples in a roasting pan of cold water, to slow the cooking down.

4 medium-sized tart green apples
½ cup dried figs, chopped roughly
1 Tbsp golden raisins
3 Tbsps honey
Yogurt, custard, or cream

Preheat an oven to 350°F. Carefully remove the cores from the apples, either with a corer or a small, sharp knife. Make a shallow cut around each apple to prevent it from bursting during cooking, then place the fruits in a buttered ovenproof dish.

Mix the chopped figs with the raisins, then pack into the apples, pressing the mixture down with the handle of a teaspoon. Drizzle the honey over the apples then pour half a cup of water into the bottom of the dish. Bake the apples in the preheated oven for about 45 minutes, until just tender—test them with the tip of a sharp knife. Do not overcook, or the apples will collapse.

Serve with yogurt, custard, or cream.

Soft Fruits with Lime Mascarpone

Serves 4

When soft fruits such as peaches and raspberries are in season and sold fully ripened, oozing flavour and juiciness, I see no reason to dress them up. However, for something just a little more special, I serve them with a rich and wicked lime-flavored cream, mixed with toasted nuts.

⅓ cup hazelnuts or almonds
4 ripe peaches
2 cups raspberries
1 cup marscarpone cheese
2 Tbsps thick plain yogurt
Grated rind and juice of 1 lime
1 Tbsp superfine sugar

Toast the nuts until golden brown in a nonstick skillet or under a broiler, then leave to cool before chopping finely.

Cut the peaches in half and remove the stones, then arrange them on individual plates with the fresh raspberries.

Beat the marscarpone until smooth, then add the yogurt, lime rind, and juice and beat again. Add sugar to taste, then fold in the chopped nuts. Serve with the prepared fruits.

Baked Bananas with Rum

Serves 4

My mother-in-law makes a similar dessert to this with lots of raw sugar—it is delicious, but I prefer to use the natural sweetness of raisins and coconut, making a lighter dessert.

4 large bananas
½ cup orange juice
2 Tbsps rum
¼ cup seedless raisins
¼ cup dried coconut
Vanilla ice cream

Preheat an oven to 375°F. Peel the bananas, cut them in half lengthways, then place in a suitable ovenproof dish that is just large enough for them. Mix the orange juice and rum together, then pour them over the bananas and sprinkle with the raisins and coconut.

Bake in the preheated oven for 15 minutes, or until the bananas are soft. Serve immediately with a scoop of vanilla ice cream.

Soft Fruits with Lime Mascarpone ▶

desserts

breads, cakes, and cookies

High-fiber baking is quite different from baking with refined white flour. Bran tends to absorb liquid and, as the whole-wheat kernel with all the bran is ground for whole-wheat flour, I find it necessary to add more liquid than I would with white flour. I notice it especially with cakes and quick breads.

Different flours always have different characteristics and liquid absorption rates, so even if you always use the same brand, be prepared to check a mixture and adjust the liquid if necessary. This particularly applies to bread making. It is easy to add more, but taking away is difficult, so always add the measured amount gradually. I like to bake with stone-ground or organic flours, both of which produce silky doughs. Again, the water absorption rate of these flours tends to be different from regular whole-wheat flour.

I refer to fine whole-wheat flour in several of my recipes. This is now widely available and should be used for pastry, cakes and cookies, sauces, and batters. It is often labelled "for cakes and pastry" on the bag and has revolutionised high-fiber baking, producing lighter results. There is little point in sifting any whole-wheat flour, as you will simply remove the bran from it.

These baking recipes have all been selected for their fiber content, but that does not mean that they are suitable for eating all day long! The cakes and cookies are still high in calories and should be eaten as a treat rather than as a basic part of your diet. Homemade whole-wheat bread is far more filling than commercial bread, so you should require less of it.

Pumpkin and Cheese Bread

Makes 1 loaf

Once you've bought a pumpkin it is a good idea to have a number of recipes to use up the flesh. Pumpkin purée adds an extra moistness to the loaf which is further flavored with a little grated Cheddar cheese.

    2½ cups whole-wheat bread flour
    1 tsp salt
    1 package active dry yeast
    1 Tbsp olive oil
    1 cup thick pumpkin purée
    1 cup warm water
    1 cup grated Cheddar cheese

Place the flour and salt in a large bowl and stir in the yeast. Make a well in the center and add the oil and pumpkin purée, then mix to a manageable dough with the water. Turn onto a lightly floured surface and knead thoroughly for about 10 minutes until elastic. Return the dough to the bowl, cover, and leave in a warm place for about 1 hour, until doubled in size.

Punch down the dough, kneading it lightly to incorporate the grated cheese. Shape into a round and place on a lightly greased baking sheet, then cover the dough and leave for a further 40 minutes until well risen.

Preheat an oven to 425°F. Scatter a little whole-wheat flour over the loaf then bake for 35–40 minutes. Cool on a wire rack.

Barley and Rye Bread

Makes 1 loaf

This is a mixed grain loaf, the two more unusual flours being combined with regular whole-wheat flour to make a lighter loaf. Neither barley or rye flours make a loaf that rises as much as a standard whole-wheat loaf, so it is essential to use a mix to obtain a reasonable rise. Barley flour is slightly sweet and combines well with the more sour flavor of the rye. More yeast is used than is usual in this loaf to help the rising.

    1½ cups warm water
    2 cups whole-wheat flour
    2 packages active dry yeast
    1 cup barley flour
    1 cup rye flour

Place the water in a large bowl; add 1 cup of whole-wheat flour and 1 package of yeast. Blend to a smooth paste then cover and leave in a warm place for 30 minutes, until full of bubbles.

Add the barley and rye flours to the ferment along with the salt and the remaining yeast. Gradually add the remaining whole-wheat flour, using as much as necessary to produce a workable dough. Turn out onto a lightly floured surface and knead thoroughly for about 10 minutes, until smooth. This dough will not become elastic.

Shape into a loaf and place in a large, greased loaf pan. Cover and leave in a warm place for about 1 hour, until well risen.

Preheat an oven to 425°F. Scatter a little flour over the loaf and bake for 35–40 minutes, until the loaf sounds hollow when tapped. Turn out of the pan and allow to cool on a wire rack.

Pumpkin and Cheese Bread ▶

breads, cakes, and cookies

Spiced Orange Breakfast Bread

Makes 1 loaf

Many Scandinavian breads are dense in texture. This loaf, based on Swedish Limpa bread, is spiced and flavored with orange and makes a wonderful breakfast bread. It is delicious with marmalade, but an acquired taste for turkey sandwiches!

    1 cup water
    1 tsp carraway seeds
    1 Tbsp fennel seeds
    1 Tbsp clear honey
    Grated rind of 1 orange
    2 cups rye flour
    2 cups whole-wheat bread flour
    1 tsp salt
    1 package active dry yeast
    2 Tbsps olive oil

Heat the water with the spices, honey, and orange rind until the honey has dissolved and the mixture is hot but not boiling. Leave to cool until tepid.

Mix all the dry ingredients together in a large bowl and add the oil. Pour the spiced water into the flours and mix to a manageable dough, adding the juice from the orange if the mixture is too dry. Knead thoroughly until the dough is smooth—this combination of flours will not produce a soft and really stretchy dough. Return the dough to the bowl, cover, and leave in a warm place for 1 hour, until well risen.

Punch the dough down, kneading it lightly, then shape into a loaf and place in a greased loaf pan. Cover and leave for a further 40 minutes.

Preheat an oven to 425°F. Bake the loaf for 45 minutes then remove from the tin and cool on a wire rack.

Toasted Hazelnut Rye Bread

Makes 1 large loaf

This is an excellent loaf, full of taste and texture. The hazelnuts add a real crunch whilst the poppy seeds give a very grainy texture to a loaf flavored with wheat and rye flours.

    3 cups whole-wheat flour
    2 cups rye flour
    2 tsps salt
    ⅓ cup blue poppy seeds
    ⅓ cup toasted hazelnuts, chopped roughly
    1 sachet easy-blend yeast
    3 Tbsps hazelnut or olive oil
    2 cups warm water

Mix the flours, salt, poppy seeds, nuts, and yeast together in a large bowl. Add the oil and sufficient water to form a manageable dough. Turn onto a lightly floured surface and knead thoroughly for about 5 minutes, until the dough is smooth—it will not become as elastic as a pure wheat dough. Shape into a round loaf and place on a lightly oiled cookie sheet, then cover and leave in a warm place for about 1 hour, until the dough has almost doubled in size.

Preheat an oven to 425°F. Score the top of the loaf with a sharp knife, If wished, then bake for 40 minutes until the base of the loaf sounds hollow when tapped. Cool on a wire rack.

◀ Spiced Orange Breakfast Bread

Golden Raisin Scones

Makes 12

Afternoon tea is a delightful meal of sandwiches, scones and homemade cakes. However, very few people have time for it now—I'm all for it coming back into fashion. Scones, the cornerstone of the afternoon tea, are very quick to make and bake.

- 2 Tbsps butter
- 3 cups fine whole-wheat flour
- 2 tsps baking powder
- ¼ cup light brown sugar
- ½ cup golden raisins
- 1 large egg, beaten
- ⅔ cup milk, approximately

Preheat an oven to 425°F and lightly grease a large baking sheet. Blend the butter into the flour and baking powder, then stir in the sugar, and raisins. Make a well in the center and pour in the beaten egg. Mix to a soft dough with the milk.

Knead the dough on a lightly floured surface until smooth, then roll out until half an inch thick. Cut out with a 2-inch cutter and place the scones on the prepared baking sheet.

Bake for 10 minutes in the preheated oven, then cool slightly on a wire rack before serving.

Sticky Buns

Makes 8

These yeasted buns are popular throughout the country. Even when made the high-fiber way, they are utterly decadent, although totally delicious.

- 2 cups whole-wheat bread flour
- 1 package active dry yeast
- ⅔ cup warm milk
- 1 Tbsp margarine
- ½ tsp salt
- 1 egg, beaten

Filling
- ¼ cup butter or margarine
- ¼ cup light brown sugar
- 2 tsps pumpkin pie spice
- ⅔ cup currants

Place ¼ cup of flour in a small bowl with the yeast and add the warm milk. Mix to a smooth paste, then cover and leave in a warm place for 25–30 minutes until full of bubbles. Blend the margarine into the remaining flour and salt in a large bowl; make a well in the center. Beat the egg then pour it into the dry ingredients. Add the yeast sponge and mix into a manageable dough. Knead thoroughly until smooth and elastic, then return the dough to the bowl. Cover and leave in a warm place for about 1½ hours, until doubled in size.

Lightly grease an 8-inch deep, round baking pan. Melt the butter, sugar, and spice for the filling together and allow to cool slightly. Pour half the mixture into the pan and spread evenly over the base. Punch the dough down by kneading lightly then roll out into a rectangle about 12x8 inches. Spread the remaining syrup over the dough then sprinkle with the currants. Roll up, trim the ends, then cut the dough into 8 pieces. Place them in the pan with the joins towards the center. Cover and leave in a warm place for a further 40 minutes.

Preheat an oven to 375°F. Bake the buns in the preheated oven for about 25 minutes then leave in the tin to cool for 2 to 3 minutes before turning out onto a wire rack to cool.

◀ Golden Raisin Scones

Wheaty Soda Bread

Makes 1 loaf

This is my favorite soda bread. The secret of a light loaf is not to overmix—the dough should just be gathered together and never kneaded.

    3 cups whole-wheat flour
    ¾ cup bran
    Pinch of salt
    2 tsps baking soda
    1 Tbsp light brown sugar
    2 cups buttermilk

Preheat an oven to 400°F and lightly grease a 7-inch deep, round cake pan.

Mix together all the dry ingredients then add the buttermilk and mix quickly with a broad bladed knife. Turn the dough out of the bowl and bring it together gently with your hands—do not actually knead the dough or overwork it, as this will make the bread heavy. Form into a rough round and place in the prepared cake pan.

Bake the soda bread in the preheated oven for 40 minutes, then turn out and cool on a wire rack. Eat the soda bread on the day it is baked.

Malted Grain Bread

Makes 2 large loaves

Malted grain flour gives a loaf of varied textures, the grains adding crunch to a soft, moist crumb. This method of breadmaking, known professionally as a flying ferment, is excellent for beginners as it encourages you to keep adding flour until the correct texture is achieved, giving a dough that is easy to handle. The water is the measured ingredient; the amount of flour required may alter from batch to batch.

    4 cups tepid water
    8–8½ cups malted grain flour
    2 packages active dry yeast
    1 Tbsp salt
    ¼ cup olive oil (optional)

Place the water in a large bowl—use the mixer bowl if you intend to knead the dough by machine. Scatter 3 cups of flour over the surface of the water with the yeast, then mix to a smooth creamy paste. Cover and leave in a warm place for about 30 minutes, until very frothy.

Add the salt and oil to the dough, then work in the remaining flour until the dough is easily manageable and does not stick to the work surface. Knead thoroughly for about 10 minutes until smooth and fairly elastic, then divide the dough into two and shape into loaves. Place the loaves either on floured baking sheets or in lightly greased loaf pans. The dough should just over half fill the loaf pans. Cover and leave in a warm place for about 40 minutes, until almost doubled in size.

Preheat an oven to 425°F. Scatter a little extra flour over the loaves then bake in the preheated oven for 45 minutes, or until the base sounds hollow when tapped. Cool on a wire rack.

▲ Malted Grain Bread

Pear and Banana Bread

Makes 1 large loaf

A moist loaf to slice and butter. The bananas sweeten the loaf, giving a soft texture, and the dried pears make a welcome change from an apple flavoring. Other fruits can be used in the same recipe, but this combination is my favorite.

3 cups fine whole-wheat flour
¾ cup bran
1½ tsps baking soda
1 tsp baking powder
Pinch of salt
⅓ cup light brown sugar
¼ cup dried pears, roughly chopped
¾ cup mashed banana (about 2 medium fruits)
1 large egg, beaten
2 cups buttermilk

Preheat an oven to 350°F and lightly grease a large loaf pan.

Place all the dry ingredients in a bowl and mix together, adding the chopped pears. Make a well in the center and add the banana. Beat the egg into the buttermilk, then pour it over the banana and mix together briefly—this is like a soda bread and should not be overworked.

Spoon the mixture into the prepared pan then bake in the preheated oven for 1 hour, or until a toothpick inserted into the loaf comes out clean. Cool in the pan for a few minutes then turn out onto a wire rack to cool completely .

Bran Teabread

Makes 1 loaf

A teabread is a moist, semisweet loaf that is usually served sliced and buttered, although seldom with jam or honey. I use tea to soak the fruits, although this is not essential. The mixture is very wet when it goes into the oven and is usually frothing. Don't worry—this is how it should be!

1 cup mixed dried fruit
1 cup cold tea
½ cup light brown sugar
¼ cup margarine
¼ cup orange marmalade
1 cup fine whole-wheat flour
1 tsp baking powder
1 tsp baking soda
1 tsp pumpkin pie spice
Pinch of salt
1 cup All-Bran cereal
1 egg, beaten

Preheat an oven to 350°F and lightly grease a large loaf pan. Place the cake fruits, tea, sugar, margarine, and marmalade in a pan and heat gently until the sugar has dissolved and the margarine melted, then leave to cool.

Mix the dry ingredients together in a large bowl and make a well in the center. Beat the egg and add it to the fruit mixture, then pour into the dry ingredients and mix thoroughly and quickly. Pour immediately into the prepared loaf pan. Bake in the preheated oven for 50–60 minutes, until a toothpick inserted into the loaf comes out clean.

Cool the teabread on a wire rack. Serve sliced and lightly buttered.

Bran Teabread ▶

Whole-wheat Drop Scones

Makes about 12

Sometimes called Scotch pancakes, these are quick to make and delcious served with butter and jam or honey. Serve them cold or keep them warm in a clean dish towel while cooking the remaining mixture. Whole-wheat drop scones are more substantial than those made with white flour.

> ⅔ cup fine whole-wheat flour
> 1 tsp baking powder
> Pinch of salt
> 1 large egg, beaten
> ⅔ cup milk, or milk and water mixed

Mix the flour, baking powder, and salt together in a bowl and make a well in the center. Beat the egg with the milk, add it to the flour, and beat to a smooth, thick batter.

Heat a heavy skillet until evenly hot then drop dessertspoonfuls of the mixture onto the surface, allowing room for them to spread slightly. Turn the scones after a minute or so, when bubbles begin to rise to the surface. Cook for a further 1 to 2 minutes then serve.

Quick Onion and Nut Loaf

Makes 1 loaf

Quick breads are often very like scone doughs but this one, being more highly seasoned than most, makes a very good loaf to serve with soups and chowders—a Saturday lunchtime bread. It may also be baked in a flat, round pan, in which case reduce the cooking time to about 30 minutes.

> 2 cups fine whole-wheat flour
> 2 tsps baking powder
> ½ tsp salt
> 1 Tbsp margarine
> 2 Tbsps roughly chopped parsley
> ½ cup coarsely grated onion
> ½ cup pecan nuts, chopped roughly
> 1 large egg, beaten
> 1 tsp Dijon or yellow mustard
> 1 cup milk

Preheat an oven to 375°F and lightly grease a small loaf pan.

Mix all the dry ingredients together in a bowl, then blend in the margarine. Stir in the parsley, onion, and pecans. Beat the egg with the mustard then add to the milk. Pour the liquid into the flour and mix to a stiff, wet batter. Pile the mixture into the prepared loaf pan—it will almost fill it—and smooth the top.

Bake in the preheated oven for 45–50 minutes, until set and lightly browned. Cool for a few minutes in the pan then turn out onto a wire rack to cool.

Quick Onion and Nut Loaf ▶

Blueberry and
Pecan Bran Muffins

Makes 6

Muffins are quick to mix and make an excellent breakfast dish when freshly baked. These will not rise as much as muffins made with white flour, but they are light in texture and full of flavor. The mix is slightly wetter than you might expect, but the bran absorbs the extra moisture.

¼ cup butter
1 large egg, beaten
½ cup milk
¼ cup light brown sugar
¾ cup fine whole-wheat flour
½ cup bran
1½ tsps baking powder
¾ cup blueberries
⅓ cup pecans, chopped finely

Preheat oven to 400°F and double-line 6 deep muffin pans with paper muffin cups. Melt the butter and leave it to cool slightly. Beat the egg with the milk, add the sugar, and leave to stand until needed.

Mix all the dry ingredients together in a bowl and add the blueberries and chopped nuts. Mix the butter with the milk and egg then pour into the bowl and mix quickly and lightly—this should take no more than a few seconds. Do not beat the mixture, which will seem rather wet.

Divide the mixture between the 6 prepared muffin cups and bake immediately in the preheated oven for 30 minutes. Cool briefly on a wire rack and serve warm.

Rock
Buns

Makes 15–18

Rock buns always remind me of home—they were one of my mother's best recipes. They may be cooked on a baking sheet, but I do them in muffin tins. I always use raw sugar for rock buns—I like the texture it gives.

½ cup butter or margarine
2 cups fine whole-wheat flour
1 heaping tsp baking powder
Pinch of salt
1–2 tsps pumpkin pie spice
1 cup mixed fruits such as golden raisins, currants
1 egg, beaten
⅓ cup milk

Preheat an oven to 400°F and lightly grease some muffin tins. Blend the butter into the flour, baking powder, salt, and spice in a bowl until the mixture resembles fine breadcrumbs. Stir in the fruit, then add the beaten egg and the milk and mix to a stiff dough.

Place spoonfuls of mixture in the prepared tins then bake in the preheated oven for 20–25 minutes. Cool on a wire rack.

◀ Blueberry and Pecan Bran Muffins

Creamed Corn Cornbread

Makes 1 large loaf

This is my favourite cornbread recipe—it is sweet yet savory and is just as good as a lunchtime snack or in place of potatoes, rice, or pasta with a meal.

  1 cup fine yellow cornmeal
  1 cup fine whole-wheat flour
  2½ tsps baking powder
  1 Tbsp light brown sugar
  2 Tbsps dried sweet bell pepper flakes or
     1 Tbsp dried chile flakes (optional)
  ½ tsp salt
  3 large eggs, separated
  15-oz can creamed corn
  ⅔ cup heavy cream
  ½ cup butter, melted

Preheat an oven to 375°F and lightly grease an 8 or 9-inch deep, round cake pan.

Mix all the dry ingredients together in a large bowl. Separate the eggs and combine the yolks with the remaining ingredients. Whisk the egg whites until stiff. Beat the corn mixture into the dry ingredients until well mixed, then fold the egg white through the mixture until evenly blended. Pour into the prepared cake pan and bake in the preheated oven for 45 minutes, until lightly browned and set.

Carefully remove the cornbread from the pan then allow it to cool slightly before serving warm. It may also be served hot, straight from the oven, as part of a meal.

Molasses Cornbread

Makes 1 loaf

Cornmeal, like barley and rye flours, does not rise as much as wheat flour because it does not have the same gluten content. It does, however, make a good all-purpose loaf when mixed with wheat flour, although the texture is a little denser. I prefer this loaf to a cornbread raised with baking powder.

  ¼ cup molasses
  ¼ cup olive oil
  1¼ cups milk
  2½ cups whole-wheat flour
  2 cups cornmeal
  2 tsps salt
  2 packages active dry yeast

Heat the molasses, oil, and milk together until the molasses has blended with the other ingredients. Remove from the heat and allow to cool. Mix the flours, salt, and yeast together in a large bowl and make a well in the center. Pour in the cooled molasses mixture then mix to a manageable dough.

Knead thoroughly until smooth—this dough will not become elastic. Shape into a loaf and place in a large, greased loaf pan, then cover and leave in a warm place for 1½ hours, until risen just above the top of the loaf pan.

Preheat an oven to 425°F while the dough is rising. Scatter a little extra cornmeal over the loaf then bake in the preheated oven for 35 minutes, or until the base of the loaf sounds hollow when tapped. Cool on a wire rack.

breads, cakes, and cookies

◄ Creamed Corn Cornbread

Grant Loaves

Makes 3 loaves

This bread bears the name of Doris Grant, a whole food campaigner who perfected a yeasted loaf prepared with no kneading—you just mix it, prove it, and bake it. It works very well, despite flying in the face of nearly all baking conventions! I have based this on a recipe given to me by the cookery writer Katie Stewart and the addition of seeds and nuts was the idea of Jeremy Ashpool, a local restaurateur.

- 8 cups stone-ground whole-wheat flour
- 2 tsps salt
- 2 packages active dry yeast
- 1 cup chopped walnuts, pumpkin, and sunflower seeds, mixed
- 5 cups tepid water
- 2 tsps molasses

Lightly grease three large loaf pans. Have the flour, mixing bowl, and loaf pans warm, especially in cold weather—this is a quick loaf to mix and cook, but it does require warmth.

Place the flour, salt, yeast, nuts, and seeds in a large, warm bowl and mix well. Add the molasses to the warm water then whisk until blended. Make a large well in the center of the flour, then add the water. Mix with a wooden spoon, scraping the flour from the edge of the bowl into the water. Continue mixing until a dough is formed, then mix with your hand until it leaves the sides of the bowl. Using your hand is the best way to judge the consistency—the dough should be sticky but not wet.

Turn onto a very lightly floured surface and divide into 3—the dough will be much softer and stickier than a regular dough. Shape roughly and place in the loaf pans. Cover, then leave in a warm place for about 30–40 minutes, until the dough has risen slightly. Meanwhile, preheat an oven to 400°F.

Bake the loaves for 35–40 minutes, until the bases sound hollow when tapped. Cool on a wire rack.

Chapatis

Makes 6

These Indian flat breads are very easy to make. They are cooked on a griddle or in a dry skillet. Do not overcook as they will become hard.

- 1 Tbsp butter
- 1 cup fine whole-wheat flour
- Good pinch of salt
- ⅓ cup warm water

Blend the butter into the flour and salt then mix to a soft dough with the water—add the liquid gradually as the amount required depends on the flour being used. Turn onto a floured surface and knead until smooth and pliable. Return the dough to the bowl, then cover and leave in a warm place for 30 minutes.

Divide the dough into 6 pieces, then roll them into balls. Dip in a little extra flour, then roll out into circles approximately 6 inches in diameter.

Heat a gridle or a nonstick skillet until evenly hot, then cook the chapatis for about 30 seconds on each side—turn them when brown spots start to appear on the surface. Keep the cooked breads warm in a clean dish towel until all the chapatis are cooked. Serve warm.

Chapatis ▶

Light Rye Sourdough

Makes 1 loaf

I call this a light rye sourdough because most rye breads, including the black breads of northern Europe, are very heavy. This loaf is made with a mixture of rye and whole-wheat flours and begins with an overnight starter to create the slightly sour taste of the bread.

    2 cups tepid milk
    1 tsp salt
    3½ cups whole-wheat bread flour
    2 packages active dry yeast
    2½ cups rye flour
    1 Tbsp salt

Place the milk in a large bowl, then stir in 2 cups of whole-wheat flour and 1 package of yeast. Blend until smooth, then cover and leave in a warm place for 14 hours—this is best done overnight.

Mix the rye flour, salt, and remaining yeast into the mixture and add as much of the whole-wheat flour as necessary to give a manageable dough. Turn onto a lightly floured surface and knead thoroughly until smooth—the dough will not become very elastic.

Shape into a round loaf and place on a floured baking sheet, or shape and place in a greased loaf pan. Cover and leave in a warm place for about 1 hour, until well risen.

Preheat an oven to 425°F. Bake the loaf for 20 minutes, then reduce the temperature to 375°F and continue cooking for a further 20 minutes. Turn the loaf out onto a wire rack to cool.

Bran Bread

Makes 1 loaf

I have often made bread with natural bran, but I am never really satisfied with the result—it gets very dark in color and is not all that attractive to look at. This loaf has extra bran added in the form of All-Bran cereal, and works much better than any other bran loaf I have tried.

    2½ cups whole-wheat bread flour
    1 tsp salt
    ½ cup All-Bran cereal
    1 sachet easy-blend dried yeast
    2 Tbsps oil
    1½ cups warm milk and water, mixed

Place the flour, salt, and All-Bran in a bowl; stir in the yeast. Add the oil, then add sufficient milk and water mixture to give a soft, manageable dough. You may find that you need a little extra liquid— the All-Bran will absorb quite a lot.

Turn onto a floured surface and knead thoroughly for about 10 minutes until smooth. Shape into a round loaf and place on a lightly greased baking sheet. Cover and leave in a warm place for about 1 hour, until well risen.

Preheat an oven to 425°F. Press a little extra All-Bran lightly into the top of the loaf, then bake for 30–35 minutes. The base of the loaf should sound hollow. Transfer to a wire rack to cool.

◀ Bran Bread

breads, cakes, and cookies

Whole-wheat Morning Rolls

Makes 18

This is an overnight dough to make creamy, soft rolls in time for breakfast. There is nothing better than waking up to the smell of freshly baking bread—a marvellous way to impress your guests.

Overnight dough
2½ cups warm water
3 cups whole-wheat bread flour
1 Tbsp salt
1 package active dry yeast

Morning dough
1 package active dry yeast
¾ cup warm water
3½ cups whole-wheat bread flour
¼ cup margarine
1 tsp light brown sugar

Place the water for the overnight dough in a large bowl. Add the flour, salt, and yeast and mix lightly—do not beat or knead. Cover and leave overnight at room temperature.

In the morning, add all the remaining ingredients to the bowl and mix to a manageable dough; the margarine will be incorporated during the mixing. Turn out onto a floured surface and knead well for about 10 minutes until smooth and elastic.

Divide the dough into 18 pieces and shape them into rolls. Place them on lightly greased baking sheets, quite close together so that they grow into each other and form a broken crust. Cover and leave in a warm place for 30 minutes to rise.

Preheat an oven to 425°F. Bake the rolls for about 20 minutes. The bases will sound hollow when tapped, but the tops of the rolls will only brown slightly and remain soft. Cool on a wire rack.

Whole-wheat Cheese Burger Rolls

Makes 8

Burger rolls or baps are almost inextricably linked with hamburgers—a soft roll of the perfect shape for serving with meat and salad. They do, however, also make excellent sandwich rolls, being soft in texture and able to take more filling than the typical bread roll. I like to add some white flour to this mixture, which should be soft and silky.

¼ cup lard
2½ cups whole-wheat bread flour
1 cup flour
1 tsp salt
1 package active dry yeast
1 cup warm milk and water, mixed
¼ cup sunflower seeds
½ cup grated Cheddar cheese

Blend the lard into the flours and salt in a large bowl. Stir in the yeast then mix to a manageable dough with the warm liquid, adding a little extra if necessary. Knead thoroughly on a lightly floured surface until soft and elastic, then return the dough to the bowl, cover, and leave in a warm place for about 1½ hours, until doubled in size.

Punch the dough down, kneading it lightly to incorporate the sunflower seeds, then divide the dough into 8 balls. Shape into rolls, then roll out until half an inch thick. Place the baps on lightly greased baking sheets, then cover and leave in a warm place for a further 30–40 minutes.

Preheat an oven to 400°F. Scatter the cheese over the baps then bake in the preheated oven for 15–20 minutes. Transfer to a wire rack to cool.

Whole-wheat Morning Rolls ▶

Wild Rice Bread

Makes 1 loaf

In many countries, where wild rice is an expensive luxury, it would seem crazy to put it into bread! However, it makes a deliciously moist loaf which is especially good with goat's cheese.

½ cup wild rice
2½ cups water
2 Tbsps molasses
2 Tbsps olive oil
1¼ cups fine whole-wheat flour
2 tsps baking powder
½ tsp salt
2 Tbsps freshly chopped chives
½ cup walnut pieces, roughly chopped
1 large egg, beaten

Bring the rice to a boil in the water, then cover the pan and cook for 45 minutes, until the rice has nearly absorbed the water and the grains have split. Stir the molasses into the rice, then leave to cool for 30 minutes.

Preheat an oven to 325°F and lightly grease a large loaf pan. Add the oil to the rice, then beat in the flour, baking powder, salt, chives, and walnuts. Beat the egg into the mixture then turn it into the prepared loaf pan. Smooth the top and bake in the preheated oven for 1 hour, or until a toothpick inserted into the loaf comes out clean.

Loosen the loaf in the pan, then turn it out carefully onto a wire rack to cool. Serve with soft goat's cheese or a cheese of your choice.

Whole-wheat Honey and Pecan Bread

Makes 1 loaf

This is a quick-mix yeasted loaf to slice and serve buttered, with jam or honey.

3 cups whole-wheat bread flour
1 cup wheat germ
½ tsp salt
1 package active dry yeast
¾ cup raisins
¾ cup toasted hazelnuts, roughly chopped
2 Tbsps sunflower oil
¼ cup honey
1–1½ cups warm water

Mix all the dry ingredients together in a large bowl and make a well in the center. Add the oil, honey, and 1 cup warm water, then mix to form a manageable dough, adding extra water as necessary. Do not add too much water or the dough will become very sticky.

Turn the dough out onto a lightly floured surface then knead thoroughly until smooth. Shape into a loaf and place in a large, greased loaf pan—the dough should just over half fill the pan. Cover and leave in a warm place for about an hour, until well risen.

Preheat an oven to 425°F. Bake the loaf for 10 minutes then reduce the temperature to 400°F and continue cooking for a further 30–35 minutes. Cool on a wire rack.

Serve the loaf sliced and buttered.

◀ Wild Rice Bread

Cheese and Walnut Scone Round

Serves 4–8

Scones are quick and easy to prepare and cook, the perfect accompaniment to soups, stews, or a bedtime drink. This mixture is baked in one large round, cutting the preparation time to an absolute minimum.

    1 stick butter
    2 cups fine whole-wheat flour
    2 tsps baking powder
    Pinch of salt
    ½ cup walnuts, roughly chopped
    1 cup grated Cheddar cheese
    1 large egg, beaten
    ½ cup milk

Preheat an oven to 425°F and lightly oil a cookie sheet.

Blend the butter into the flour, baking powder, and salt, then stir in the nuts and cheese. Beat the egg with the milk then use to mix to a soft but manageable dough.

Turn onto a lightly floured surface then knead lightly until smooth. Shape the dough into a round about 1 inch thick, and mark into eight. Bake on the cookie sheet for 20–25 minutes. Cool for at least 10 minutes before eating to avoid indigestion!

breads, cakes, and cookies

Date Flapjack

Serves 8–10

This is one of my favorite cakes for both the home cake plate and the never-ending round of bake sales for worthy causes! It is quick to make and bake, looks terrific and tastes delicious. It does, however, contain a lot of calories and should be saved for occasional treats!

    2 cups dried dates, roughly chopped
    ⅔ cup water
    1 tsp vanilla extract
    ¾ cup butter
    2 cups rolled oats
    1 cup whole-wheat flour
    1 cup light brown sugar

Preheat an oven to 350°F and line a deep 8-inch baking pan. Place the dates and water in a pan and cook slowly until the dates are soft, the water is slightly reduced, and the mixture can be beaten into a thick purée. Add the vanilla then set the mixture aside until needed.

Melt the butter in a pan then stir in all the remaining ingredients. Press half the mixture into the bottom of the prepared pan, then top it with the date mixture before pressing the remaining oat mixture over the dates. Smooth the top then bake in the preheated oven for 30 minutes.

Mark into portions while still warm then leave to cool completely before slicing. Store in an airtight container.

Date Flapjack ▶

breads, cakes, and cookies

Fig Cake

Makes 1 cake

For fig lovers everywhere! This is a cross between a cake and a cookie. There is no sugar added to the figs, and the orange juice prevents the mixture from being too sweet.

1½ cups roughly chopped, ready-to-eat dried figs
Grated rind and juice of 1 orange

2 cups fine whole-wheat flour
Pinch of salt
⅓ cup soft brown sugar
¾ stick butter
1 large egg, beaten

Place the figs, orange rind, and juice in a pan and cook slowly for 10–15 minutes until soft. Mash together gently with a wooden spoon then set aside until needed.

Blend the butter into the flour, salt, and sugar. Add the egg and sufficient water to mix to a manageable dough. Roll out half the mixture and press into the bottom of an 8-inch baking pan with a loose bottom, then spread with the figs. Roll the remaining dough into a circle just a little smaller than the tin, then place over the figs and press down firmly sealing the two crusts together. Chill the fig cake while preheating the oven.

Preheat an oven to 375°F. Bake the cake for 30 minutes, or until the dough is set. Mark into 8 to 10 segments while still warm, then cut when completely cold.

▲ Fig Cake

Parkin

Makes 1 cake

Parkin is similar to gingerbread in taste but has a much rougher texture because it is made with pinhead or Irish oatmeal (pinhead oatmeal gives a slightly finer texture). I always think that it is better a day or two after it has been made. As with all melting-method cakes, you must be careful not to allow the treacle mixture to boil, or the Parkin will develop a tough crust.

¾ cup black treacle or molasses
⅓ cup light brown sugar
½ cup margarine
1¼ cups fine whole-wheat flour
2 tsps baking powder
Pinch of salt
1 cup pinhead or Irish oatmeal
2 large eggs, beaten
⅔ cup milk to mix (approx)

Preheat oven to 325°F and line an 11x7-inch tin with baking parchment.

Heat the treacle, sugar, and margarine together gently until the margarine has melted and the sugar dissolved. Leave to cool slightly. Mix all the dry ingredients together in a large bowl and make a well in the center. Add the beaten eggs to the treacle mix then pour into the dry ingredients and mix thoroughly adding sufficient milk to give a soft, runny consistency.

Pour the Parkin quickly into the prepared tin and bake in the preheated oven for 1 hour. Carefully transfer onto a wire rack to cool. Cut into squares when cold and store in an airtight container until required.

Granola Cookies

These sweet cookies are very quick to make, but they must be chilled before baking or they will spread too much in the oven. The honey binds the mixture together; no egg is used. Knead the dough well to produce light cookies.

> ½ cup butter or margarine
> ½ cup light brown sugar
> ¼ cup honey
> 2 cups granola
> ½ cup fine whole-wheat flour

Cream the butter and sugar together until pale and fluffy, then add the honey and beat thoroughly again. Work in the granola and flour to give a stiff dough which is only slightly sticky, then turn out onto a lightly floured surface and knead firmly until the dough is easily manageable. Form into a sausage shape, about 12 inches long, then cover in plastic wrap and chill in the refrigerator for at least 30 minutes.

Preheat an oven to 350°F and lightly grease 2 baking sheets. Cut the cookie dough into 20 pieces, form into balls, then flatten slightly and place on the prepared baking sheets. Bake in the preheated oven for 12–15 minutes, until lightly browned. Leave the cookies to cool slightly on the baking sheets until firm enough to transfer to a wire rack to cool competely.

Store in an airtight container or cookie jar.

Whole-wheat Sandwich Loaf

Makes 2 large loaves

This is the basic everyday bread that we eat at home. Sometimes I use all whole-wheat flour, but I generally prefer to use one third white flour, which gives a slightly lighter loaf. Using active dry yeast means that the dough can be kneaded only once and shaped, cutting down on the time required to make the loaves.

> 6 cups whole-wheat bread flour
> 2 cups strong white flour
> 1 Tbsp salt
> 2 packages active dry yeast
> ¼ cup olive oil
> 4 cups tepid water, approximately

Place all the dry ingredients in a large bowl and mix in the yeast. Add the oil and most of the water, then mix to a workable dough, adding the remaining water if necessary. Turn out onto a floured surface and knead thoroughly for about 10 minutes until smooth and fairly elastic.

Divide the dough into 2 and shape into loaves. Place the loaves either on floured baking sheets or in lightly greased loaf pans. The dough should just over half fill the loaf pans. Cover and leave in a warm place for about 40 minutes, until well risen and almost doubled in size.

Preheat oven to 425°F. Scatter a little extra flour over the loaves then bake in the preheated oven for 45 minutes, or until the bases sound hollow when tapped. Cool on a wire rack.

Granola Cookies ▶

Potato Griddle Cakes

Makes about 20

Based on an old Irish recipe, this is a good way of using up leftover mashed potatoes—however, warm potato makes lighter scones so heat the potato through (a microwave works well) before mixing the dough.

1½ cups mashed potato
½ tsp salt
1 Tbsp margarine or butter
½ cup fine whole-wheat flour

Mix the mashed potato with the salt and margarine then add sufficient flour to produce a stiff dough. Knead lightly on a floured surface then roll out to a quarter-inch thickness. Cut into 2-inch rounds.

Preheat a griddle or heavy skillet then cook the scones for 4–5 minutes, until lightly browned on both sides. Turn once during cooking. Serve spread with butter or margarine.

Banana Cornmeal Muffins

Makes 12

These muffins have an unusual texture but are deliciously light. The bananas add a moist sweetness but do not give too strong a flavor; the ginger is just in the background.

1 cup fine whole-wheat flour
½ cup fine cornmeal
½ cup light brown sugar
1½ tsps baking powder
½ tsp baking soda
Pinch of salt
1 tsp ground ginger
¾ cup roughly mashed banana (3 medium fruits)
2 large eggs, beaten
1 cup sour cream
1 Tbsp margarine or butter, melted

Preheat an oven to 350°F and line 12 muffin pans with paper cases.

Mix all the dry ingredients together in a bowl and add the bananas. Beat the eggs with the sour cream and add the melted margarine. Pour into the dry ingredients and work quickly until the mixture is just combined together—do not beat.

Divide the mixture between the muffin pans then bake in the preheated oven for 25 minutes, until a toothpick inserted into the muffins comes out clean. Cool briefly on a wire rack. Serve warm.

◀ Potato Griddle Cakes

Raisin and Pineapple Cake

Makes 1 medium cake

I have never been a fan of very rich fruitcakes—I even make my Christmas cake using this blended recipe, which can easily be dressed up by adding some sherry to the cake mix, along with dried peaches or pineapple. This is an everyday fruitcake, embellished with unusual dried fruit—raisins and currants would be just as good.

1 cup mixed fruits (dried pineapple, golden raisins, dried cranberries, etc.)
½ cup pineapple or orange juice
¾ cup margarine or butter
2 cups fine whole-wheat flour
2 tsps baking powder
Pinch of salt
1 tsp ground ginger
½ cup light brown sugar
2 large eggs, beaten

Soak the fruits in the fruit juice for 10 minutes. Preheat an oven to 350°F and lightly grease a 7-inch deep, round cake pan.

Blend the butter into the flour, baking powder, salt, and ginger in a bowl until the mixture resembles fine bread crumbs. Stir in the sugar, then add the fruits and juice and the beaten eggs. Mix to a soft dropping consistency, adding a little extra fruit juice or milk as required, then spoon the mixture into the prepared cake pan and smooth the top.

until the cake stops "singing"—yes, go on, listen to it—and a toothpick inserted into the center comes out clean.

Cool slightly in the pan then turn out carefully onto a wire rack to cool completely.

Raisin and Pineapple Cake ▶

Zucchini and Raisin Cake

Makes 1 large cake

This cake was inspired by a conventional passion cake made with carrots, but is much more moist. It may be eaten plain, spread with butter icing or cream cheese frosting.

1⅔ cups fine whole-wheat flour
1 tsp baking soda
2 tsps baking powder
1 tsp salt
1 tsp ground ginger
1 cup soft brown sugar
⅔ cup raisins or golden raisins
1 cup grated zucchini, closely packed
1 cup grated carrot
⅔ cup natural yogurt
3 large eggs, beaten
⅔ cup corn oil

Preheat an oven to 350°F, and line a 9-inch round cake pan with baking parchment.

Place the flour, baking soda, baking powder, ginger, sugar, and raisins in a bowl then mix in the zucchini and carrot. Add the yogurt with the eggs, then finally add the oil. Mix to a thick batter then beat vigorously for 1 minute. Pour the mixture into the prepared tin, then bake in the preheated oven for 1 hour, until a toothpick inserted into the mixture comes out clean. Cool slightly, then turn out onto a wire rack and leave until completely cold.

Cranberry and Coffee Cake

Makes 1 cake

This is a very light sponge cake made with oil, flavored with coffee, with dried cranberries folded into the mixture. It may be served as a plain sponge cake or decorated with whipped cream and fresh fruits, such as apricots, blueberries, or cherries, or whatever fruits are in season.

  3 large eggs
  ½ cup light brown sugar
  ⅔ cup fine whole-wheat flour
  1 Tbsp sunflower oil
  1 tsp coffee essence
  ⅓ cup dried cranberries, chopped roughly

  Whipped cream and fresh fruit (optional)

Preheat an oven to 375°F then lightly grease an 8 to 9-inch cake pan and line the base with baking parchment.

Whisk the eggs and sugar together until pale and fluffy—this is best done in an electric mixer and may take up to 10 minutes. Fold in the flour a few spoonfuls at a time, then add the oil and essence, drizzling them down the side of the bowl. Finally, add the cranberries, folding in lightly. Transfer the mixture immediately to the prepared cake pan and bake in the preheated oven for 20–25 minutes, until the mixture springs back when pressed lightly and shrinks away from the sides of the tin.

Turn the cake out onto a wire rack to cool completely. Decorate with fruit and whipped cream, if wished, then serve sliced.

Honey and Ginger Cake

Makes 1 loaf cake

Ginger cakes are usualy made with corn syrup or molasses—this one has a milder flavor because it is made with honey. It is one of our favorite cakes.

  ½ cup margarine
  ½ cup honey
  ½ cup light brown sugar
  2 cups fine whole-wheat flour
  1½ tsps baking soda
  2 tsps ground ginger
  2 large eggs, beaten
  2 Tbsps milk

Preheat an oven to 325°F and line an 11x7-inch pan with baking parchment.

Heat the margarine, honey, and sugar together over a low heat until the margarine has melted and the sugar dissolved—do not allow the mixture to boil or the cake will become crusty. Leave to cool.

Mix the dry ingredients together in a large bowl and make a well in the center. Beat the eggs with the milk then stir into the honey mixture. Pour into the dry ingredients and mix thoroughly. Pour into the prepared pan and bake in the preheated oven for 40 minutes, or until a toothpick inserted into the cake comes out clean. Remove from the pan and cool completely on a wire rack. Wrap in foil or store in an airtight container for 1 to 2 days to allow the flavor to develop before eating.

breads, cakes, and cookies

◀ Cranberry and Coffee Cake

Rhubarb Streusel Cake

Makes 1 large cake

This may be served as either a cake or a pudding but I prefer it cold as a cake. The crumb topping gives a delicious crunch in contrast to the rhubarb, which softens into the cake mix. Apples and gooseberries are good alternatives to the rhubarb.

Streusel topping
⅓ cup butter
1 cup fine whole-wheat flour
½ tsp baking powder
½ cup raw sugar

½ cup butter or margarine
⅔ cup light brown sugar
2 large eggs, beaten
1 cup fine whole-wheat flour
1 tsp baking powder
½ tsp ground cinnamon
1 Tbsp milk
2 cups rhubarb pieces, in 2-inch lengths, fresh or canned

Preheat an oven to 350°F, then line an 8-inch deep, round cake pan with baking parchment.

First prepare the topping. Blend the butter into the flour, baking powder, and sugar until evenly distributed, then set aside. Cream the butter and sugar together until pale and fluffy then gradually add the beaten eggs. Mix the flour, baking powder, and cinnamon together, then fold it into the mixture, adding the milk to give a soft dropping consistency.

Spoon the cake mixture into the prepared tin and roughly smooth the top. Arrange the rhubarb over the sponge then cover with the topping mixture, spreading it evenly.

Bake the cake in the preheated oven for 1 hour, or until a toothpick inserted into the cake comes out clean. Leave in the tin for 2 to 3 minutes, then remove the cake carefully, peel off the paper, and allow to cool completely on a wire rack.

Rhubarb Streusel Cake ▶

Apricot Granola Bars

Makes 8

A substantial snack or a light meal—these fruit granola bars are satisfying!

Filling
1 cup dried apricots, chopped finely
Grated rind and juice of 1 orange

⅓ cup margarine
⅓ cup honey
2 cups granola
½ cup fine whole-wheat flour

Preheat an oven to 375°F and lightly grease a 7-inch square cake pan.

Cook the apricots with the orange rind and juice, simmering slowly until all the orange juice has disappeared. Allow to cool until needed. Melt the margarine in a pan, add the honey, and heat gently until melted into the margarine. Stir in the granola and flour and mix well.

Press half the granola mixture into the prepared cake pan then cover with a layer of apricots. Top with the remaining granola mixture, pressing it down and smoothing the top with a metal spoon. Try to poke any raisins into the mixture so that they do not overcook.

Bake in the preheated oven for 20–25 minutes, until lightly browned. Mark into bars and allow to cool in the pan. Cut through then cool completely on a wire rack. Store in an airtight container.

◀ Apricot Granola Bars

Whole-wheat Cinnamon Cookies

Makes 18

Spicy topped sugary cookies that are perfect for dunking in coffee or hot chocolate.

½ stick butter
1 cup fine whole-wheat flour
½ a freshly grated nutmeg
⅔ cup soft brown sugar
1 medium egg, beaten

2 Tbsps Demerara sugar
1 tsp ground cinnamon

Blend the butter into the flour, nutmeg, and sugar, then bind to a dough with the beaten egg. Turn out onto floured surface and knead lightly until the dough is smooth, then cover in plastic wrap and chill for at least 30 minutes.

Preheat an oven to 400°F. Shape into 18 walnut-sized pieces, then place on greased cookie sheets and flatten slightly with a fork. Mix together the Demerara sugar and cinnamon, then sprinkle the mixture over the cookies. Bake for 12–15 minutes, swopping the trays half way through cooking if necessary. Cool on a wire rack and store in an air-tight tin.

Granola Cake

Makes 1 cake

Granola is not just a breakfast cereal—it is also a valuable ingredient for high-fiber baking. This cake should be stored for 2 or 3 days before it is eaten.

  1½ cups granola
  ½ cup light brown sugar
  ⅓ cup clear honey
  1 cup golden raisins
  1 cup unsweetened grape or orange juice
  1 cup fine whole-wheat flour
  2 tsps baking powder
  1 tsp baking soda
  2 tsps pumpkin pie spice
  1 large egg, beaten

Preheat an oven to 325°F, then grease and line a 7 x 11-inch cake pan. Heat the granola, sugar, honey, and raisins with the fruit juice until the sugar has dissolved, then leave to cool for 10 minutes.

Mix together the dry ingredients. Add the beaten egg to the granola mix, then add the dry ingredients and quickly beat into a thick, frothy paste. Pour into the prepared cake pan, lightly smooth the top, and bake in the preheated oven for 40 minutes. Cool slightly then mark into squares. Allow to cool completely on a wire rack before cutting, then store in an airtight container.

All-Butter Shortbread

Makes 1 large shortbread

The Scots are famed for their shortbreads. Usually made with bleached white flour, it is traditional to add some ground rice to the mixture to give it texture. This is not necessary when baking with whole-wheat flour, but one thing is, in my opinion, essential: the use of butter, which gives this cookie the most delicious flavor.

  ½ cup slightly softened butter
  1 cup fine whole-wheat flour
  Pinch of salt
  ⅓ cup light brown sugar

Preheat an oven to 350°F and lightly grease a 7-inch baking pan—I usually line the pan with baking parchment, although this is not essential.

Blend the butter into the flour, salt, and sugar in a bowl until the mixture resembles fine breadcrumbs. Turn into the prepared pan and press down with a broad-bladed knife. Lightly mark the shortbread into 8 portions, then prick through to the base using a fork and make a decorative edge.

Bake in the preheated oven for 25–30 minutes. Cool slightly in the pan then mark the shortbread into portions again before turning out onto a wire rack to cool. Cut through or break into portions when completely cold.

Peanut Butter Cookies

These cookies are rich! I use raw sugar in them as the flavor is less dominating and allows the peanut butter to shine through.

- ⅓ cup crunchy peanut butter
- ¼ cup margarine
- ½ cup raw sugar
- 1 large egg, beaten
- 1 cup fine whole-wheat flour
- 1 tsp baking powder

Cream together the peanut butter, margarine, and sugar then add the beaten egg. Fold in the flour and baking powder and form into a stiff dough. Turn out onto a floured surface and knead lightly. Cover in plastic wrap and chill for about 1½ hours, until firmer and easier to handle.

Preheat an oven to 350°F and lightly grease two baking sheets. Cut the dough into 18 slices and form each into a ball, then press lightly to flatten as you place them on the prepared baking sheets. Dip a fork into a little flour and press it into the tops of the cookies, then bake in the preheated oven for 15–20 minutes. Cool slightly before transferring to a wire rack to cool completely.

Carrot Cake

Makes 1 large cake

A wonderful cake to serve for everyday eating and for special occasions as part of a buffet. I am very generous with the frosting—you can't be good all the time!

- 2 cups fine whole-wheat flour
- 2 tsps baking powder
- 1 tsp baking soda
- 1 tsp salt
- 1 tsp pumpkin pie spice (optional)
- ½ cup walnut pieces, finely chopped
- 3 large eggs, beaten
- ⅔ cup mashed banana (2 medium-sized fruits)
- 1½ cups grated carrot
- ¾ cup sunflower oil

Frosting
- ¾ cup softened butter
- ¾ cup cream cheese
- 1 tsp vanilla extract
- 2½ cups icing sugar, sieved

Preheat an oven to 350°F then lightly grease a 9-inch, deep round cake pan and line it with baking parchment.

Mix all the dry ingredients together in a large bowl then add the eggs, mashed bananas, and carrots. Pour the oil into the bowl and beat thoroughly to a thick, well-blended batter. Spoon into the prepared cake pan and bake in the center of the preheated oven for about 1 hour, until a toothpick inserted into the cake comes out clean. Remove the cake carefully from the cake pan and allow to cool completely on a wire rack.

Prepare the frosting by beating together the softened butter and cream cheese until blended, then add the vanilla extract and beat again. Sift the icing sugar and beat it gradually into the cheese mixture. Spread the frosting over the cake and decorate, if wished, with finely chopped walnuts or a little extra grated carrot. Serve in thin slices.

▲ Carrot Cake

Walnut Cookies

Makes about 30

These cookies are delicious as they are, but could easily be coated with melted chocolate or a chocolate substitute such as carob. Use pecans if you prefer, but I find the slightly more bitter flavor of walnuts very good in cookies. Place the cookies far apart on the baking sheets or they may spread into each other.

½ cup butter, slightly softened
⅔ cup light brown sugar
1 large egg, beaten
1 cup fine whole-wheat flour
1 tsp baking powder
¾ cup walnut pieces, finely chopped

Cream the butter and sugar together until pale—the mixture will be slightly sticky. Add the egg and mix well, then fold in the flour and baking powder, then finally work in the nuts.

Turn the mixture out onto a lightly floured surface and knead gently to bring the dough together. Roll into a sausage shape about 12 inches long, wrap in plastic wrap, and chill for at least 1 hour, until firm enough to handle.

Preheat an oven to 350°F and lightly grease 2 or 3 baking sheets. Cut the dough into thin slices and roll them into balls about the size of a walnut. Place on the prepared baking sheets, flattening the cookies slightly with the palm of your hand. Bake for 12–15 minutes, then allow to cool slightly on the baking sheet before transferring to a wire rack to cool completely.